HOTSPOTS
TURKE
MEDITERRANEAN COAST

C000185761

Alanya, Antalya, Side, Kemer, Beldibi & Tekirova, Belek

Written by Lindsay Bennett
Front cover photography courtesy of Thomas Cook Tour Operations Ltd

Original design concept by Studio 183 Limited
Series design by the Bridgewater Book Company
Cover design/artwork by Lee Biggadike, Studio 183 Limited

Produced by the Bridgewater Book Company
The Old Candlemakers, West Street, Lewes, East Sussex BN7 2NZ, United Kingdom
www.bridgewaterbooks.co.uk
Project Editor: Emily Casey Bailey
Project Designer: Lisa McCormick

Published by Thomas Cook Publishing
A division of Thomas Cook Tour Operations Limited
PO Box 227, Units 15-16, Coningsby Road, Peterborough PE3 8SB, United Kingdom
email: books@thomascook.com
www.thomascookpublishing.com
+ 44 (0) 1733 416477

ISBN-13: 978-1-84157-534-6
ISBN-10: 1-84157-534-8

First edition © 2006 Thomas Cook Publishing
Text © 2006 Thomas Cook Publishing
Maps © 2006 Thomas Cook Publishing
Head of Thomas Cook Publishing: Chris Young
Project Editor: Diane Ashmore
Production/DTP Editor: Steven Collins

Printed and bound in Spain by Graficas Cems, Navarra, Spain

CONTENTS

SYMBOLS KEY

The following is a key to the symbols used throughout this book:

i	information office	**P**	car park	**¶**	restaurant
⊟	bus station	**⬟**	police station	**⬛**	café
✕	post office	**✈**	airport	**Y**	bar
✝	church	**↘**	tip	**◉**	fine dining
⊒	train station	**⬛**	shopping		

☎ telephone   **📠** fax   **e** email   **w** website address

a address   **🕐** opening times   **!** important

€ budget price   **€€** mid-range price   **€€€** most expensive

★ specialist interest   ★★ see if passing   ★★★ top attraction

---

INTRODUCTION
Getting to know Turkey's Mediterranean coast

CAPPADOCIA

ANAMUR

Ermenek •

Gökdere Çay

GAZIPAŞA

ALANYA

Manavgat •
SIDE •

Belek •

BELDIBI
KEMER
TEKIROVA
KUMLUCA

ELMALI •

KALE
Myra •
Kekova
Boat Trip

MEDITERRANEAN SEA

N

BULGARIA

TURKEY

SYRIA

CYPRESS/
CYPRUS

Getting to know
Turkey's Mediterranean coast

Is your idea of the perfect holiday destination long, hot sunny days? Beautiful sandy beaches? Crystal-clear seas? Friendly people? Lots to see and do, but no rush to do anything? 'Buzzing' nightlife or a quiet evening with just the buzzing of the cicadas? A touch of spice but with a few touches of home? If so, then Turkey is the place for you.

A LAND RICH IN HISTORY

'Where East and West meet' or 'the Crossroads of History' are just two ways to describe this land. Turkey stretches from the Aegean Sea in the west into the Middle East and Asia in the east, and it has been used as a land bridge for hundreds of generations. Persians, Greeks, Romans, Byzantines and Ottomans all feature strongly in its long history and have left fascinating legacies for today's holidaymakers to explore.

NATURAL BEAUTY

Not a history buff? No worries! Turkey has much more to offer. The Mediterranean region has a one of the most varied landscapes in Turkey. In the west, the 3,000 m (9,843 ft) peaks of the Taurus and Olymbos Mountains form a dramatic backdrop for the resorts, but as you travel east the mountains retreat inland, leaving a wide and dusty coastal plain. The mountains offer shelter from the harsh Siberian winds that cut across inland Turkey during the winter, giving Antalya and its close surroundings the mildest year-round climate in the country.

A VARIETY OF RESORTS

The region is anchored by three major 'mega' resorts, each with a different character. Antalya, the capital of the region, is a city with a life outside tourism and a cosmopolitan atmosphere, while Side is a pure resort town with a very mixed continental clientele. Alanya, the most easterly of the three, has two great beaches and a magnificent citadel. Outside these you will find Turkey's first purpose-built resorts – Belek

◆ *Unspoilt beaches along Turkey's Mediterranean coastline*

and Kemer being the most popular – set in the finest locations and with a great range of up-to-date sports facilities. From all these resorts a weath of excursions awaits.

EVENING ENTERTAINMENT

How to fill the balmy evenings? The large towns offer some of the most raucous nightlife of any holiday destination in Europe – great foam parties and fishbowl cocktails – while smaller resorts are the perfect locations for romantic meals and moonlit strolls on the beaches. Or you could always head to a Turkish bath for a little pampering.

The best of Turkey's Mediterranean coast

The Turkish Mediterranean offers a wealth of fantastic experiences that fill the hours from just after dawn until well after dusk.

Explore Kaleiçi in Antalya Take a daytime stroll leading to drinks overlooking the harbour as the sun sets in the medieval heart of this sophisticated resort (see page 26)

Views from the citadel at Alanya Get a bird's-eye view of the coast from the battlements of this impressive 13th-century fortress (see page 14)

Explore atmospheric Side town Where past meets present (see page 33)

Tee off at Belek You will not feel under par after a round on these excellent greens (see page 46)

The theatre at Aspendos An awe-inspiring example of Roman architecture still being used today (see page 60)

White-water rafting at Köprülü Canyon Sheer exhilaration (see page 62)

Barter for a bargain at the bazaar Shopping is theatre in Turkey, designed to both entertain and lighten your wallet

The flames of Chimaera View one of mother nature's hottest spectacles (see page 75)

Swim with the dolphins Get up close with these intelligent and beautiful sea mammals

The lost city of Termessos The 'hidden' city that thwarted Alexander the Great (see page 64)

RESORTS
Places under the sun

Alanya
miles of sand with a real castle

One of Turkey's most easterly tourist resort, Alanya, has a high rocky promontory that is one of the most dramatic along the coast. The 250 m (820 ft) high precipice has a magnificent citadel that was the focus of the town for centuries.

Flanking the promontory like long golden wings are two exceptional beaches that are the main draw as far as holidaymakers are concerned. A ribbon of hotels, bars and restaurants now fans out on either side of the town, so whichever accommodation you choose you are never far from refreshment and entertainment.

Aside from the tourist strip along the coast, restaurants and nightlife are clustered in a triangle between the harbourfront, **Işkele Caddesi** and **Hukümet Caddesi** in the shadow of the citadel. You can take a quiet meal across from the fishing boats before diving into the sometimes raucous bars and clubs that stay open until the early hours.

The main thoroughfare, **Damlataş Caddesi**, links old Alanya with the new town. Lined with trees and street cafés and boutiques, it has an atmosphere similar to that of a French boulevard. The side streets, with their small shops and market stalls, offer a total contrast – here you can bargain for that must-have souvenir among the hustle and bustle.

HISTORY

Founded as a Greek colony, Alanya became a renowned pirate base in the 2nd century BC because it was easy from here to target the ships carrying valuable cargo across the Eastern Mediterranean from Cyprus and Egypt. The Romans were not happy about this and eventually sent a naval force to crush the rebels in 67 BC.

In 44 BC Roman general and would-be emperor Mark Anthony gave the town to his lover and political ally, Cleopatra, queen of Egypt. Unfortunately for them, they were beaten by rivals within the empire and, according to legend, Cleopatra took her own life by allowing herself to be bitten by an asp (a venomous snake). The town was a southern bastion of the Christian Byzantine Empire, but was taken by the Muslim Seljuks in 1221; their first sultan put the final touches to the magnificent castle, making it his naval base and winter home.

 Alanya tourist office ⓐ Damlataş Caddesi 1
ⓣ 0242 513 1240

THINGS TO SEE & DO
Alanya Museum ★
Although the museum has the usual range of ancient remains, plus photographs of where they were found, the best part of the

museum is the collection of Ottoman relics. There is a recreation of a traditional Ottoman living room and some old farming implements in the garden. ❸ Hilmi Balci Caddesi, off Damlataş Caddesi 🕒 Open Tues–Sun 08.00–noon and 13.00–17.30, closed Mon ❶ Admission charge

Atatürk Museum ★

Atatürk, founder of the Turkish republic and national hero, made a fleeting visit to Alanya in the 1920s and stayed in this house, which is now preserved as a museum. Today, the downstairs rooms pay homage to Atatürk with photographs and documents. The upstairs part of the house may be more interesting to foreign tourists. It is furnished in the typical style of the early Turkish republic, which flourished in the 1920s and 1930s. ⓐ Hilmi Balci Caddesi 🕾 0242 513 3254 🕒 Open 08.30–noon and 13.30–17.30 ❶ Admission free

Citadel ★★★

The setting of the citadel in Alanya is one of the most dramatic in Turkey. Built high on the sheer rocky peak that separates the two beaches, it was considered impregnable in medieval times.

Ehmediye ★★

This old village within the citadel nestles around the walls of İç Kale. There is a 16th-century mosque and some atmospheric old Ottoman houses, but they are difficult to explore because of the sea of cotton and linen festooned along the alleyways. The women here used to crochet and make lace by hand and sell it to tourists. Today, most of it is machine made and even imported, although you can still buy some lovely table sets as souvenirs. There are numerous small cafés where you can enjoy a drink before you head back down into town.

İç Kale ★★★

At the very top of the peak is the Inner Castle, or İç Kale, built in 1226. This was the military and political headquarters of Seljuk leader

Alâeddin Keykubad. The walls remain almost intact and from here the panoramic views down the hill, over the town and beaches and both east and west along the Mediterranean coast are truly breathtaking. Stand on a small platform in the north-west corner. This is where prisoners were once thrown to their deaths. 🕐 Open 09.00–21.00 (summer); Tues–Sun 09.00–18.00 (winter) ❶ Admission charge

Outer Citadel ★

A total of 7 km (4 miles) of walls are draped around the slopes of the hill. These are held together by around 150 towers set at strategic lookout and entry points. The garrison lived within these lower slopes, and it included hundreds of foot soldiers and their families, blacksmiths, cooks and laundry workers. You can see the ruins of their military village on the approach road to the inner castle.

Harbour ★

The lovely inner harbour at the foot of Kızılkule is home to hundreds of small, colourful fishing and pleasure boats. You can watch the fishermen mending their nets or just relax at one of several cafés.

Tersane ★

The shipyard, or *tersane*, was erected by the Seljuks to build and repair their shipping fleet. This is said to be the only shipyard of its age still found in Turkey. ➋ On the harbour to the north of Red Tower 🕐 Open 24 hours ❶ Admission free

Kızılkule ★★

Kızılkule (Red Tower) was built as part of the harbour defences in 1226, the same year as İç Kale. The name comes from the red stone of its octagonal walls. There is a small ethnological or lifestyle museum inside, but more exciting are the views across the harbour from the top battlements. ➋ On the harbour front ☎ 0242 512 3255 🕐 Open Tues–Sun 09.00–18.00, closed Mon ❶ Admission charge

SHOPPING

 Alanya town There is a wide range of goods to be found within Alanya's main shopping area (off Damlataş Caddesi towards the harbour and around the *otogar*), but also a fair amount of T-shirts, jeans and designer rip-offs. More upmarket boutiques – particulary those selling locally produced silk, which is a speciality of the town – can be found on Damlataş Caddesi itself.

Ehmediye village In the citadel, this is the place to shop for lace and table linens, which bedeck every alleyway and shop front.

Market Held weekly, on Fridays, this is a huge affair and fills the streets around the dolmuş station.

Damlataş ★★

You can reach Damlataş, or the Cave of the Dripping Stones, from land, and it is one of the most impressive caves in the area, with spectacular stalactites and stalagmites. The constant temperature and damp air of the caves is said to be good for people with asthma. ⓐ Damlataş Caddesi ⓒ Open 10.00–sunset ⓘ Admission charge

Büyük Alanya Hamman ★

A Turkish bath with sauna, jacuzzi, hairdresser and bar – so not exactly traditional. ⓐ Damlataş Caddesi at the corner of Alaattinoğlu Sokak ⓣ 0242 511 3344 ⓘ Admission charge

Waterplanet ★

This water park has 23 slides and rides, a 350 m (383 ft) artificial river for rafting, wave pools, bars, restaurants and a discotheque. ⓐ Okurcalar Mevkii, Manavgat (30 km/19 miles from Alanya on the way to Side) ⓣ 0242 527 5164 ⓦ www.waterplanet.com.tr ⓘ Admission charge

BEACHES

Alanya's town beaches are impressive. Sitting either side of the citadel, they have been given the rather unromantic names East and West Beach. **West Beach** is the longest, at 8 km (5 miles), and this is where the vast majority of the new tourist development has taken place, a thin ribbon of hotels, restaurants and bars stretching into the distance. The beach has all the usual tourist amenities, including a full range of water sports. **East Beach** is only 3 km (2 miles) long but is still longer than the beaches at many other resorts in Turkey. It tends to be a little quieter than West Beach and attracts more local people, especially at weekends. **Cleopatra's Beach** sits in the shadow of the citadel and is the smallest of the town beaches. It does not have the level of amenities of the other two, with simple snack bars and cafés, but there are volleyball courts here, and competitions are held during the summer.

EXCURSIONS
Alarahan ★★

Hans were wayside inns built during Seljuk times for the camel and horse trains that carried goods across Asia. Alarahan was built in the 13th century at the foot of a pass through the Taurus Mountains on the banks of the River Alara by Seljuk Sultan Alâeddin Keykubad. It did not alter much until it underwent a massive renovation in the late 1990s.

It is a job well done because the architects have not messed about with the basic structure. You can still see the stables where the animals were tethered and the communal sleeping and eating chambers for the men. The building is open as a museum and café during the day, with a great sitting area on the roof. In the evenings it hosts Turkish evenings with traditional foods and dancing.

The ruins of a Byzantine fortress sit on a rocky outcrop above the *han*. There is a footpath up there, but it is not well used and the climb is steep in parts. Allow four hours if you want to attempt the trip.

◉ 39 km (24 miles) west of Alanya, inland from the main 400 coast road
🕐 Open 10.00–01.00 ❶ Admission charge

🔺 *Alanya Castle is situated high on a sheer rocky peak*

Anamur ★★

It is full-day trip to reach Anamur on the coast, but worth it for history lovers. ⓐ 110 km (68 miles) east of Alanya

Anemurium ★★

Located on a spit of land that is the southern-most tip of Turkey are the remains of Anemurium, an important late-Roman and Byzantine city, abandoned in the 7th century when Arab forces took control of Cyprus and began sacking settlements along this coast. The site has not been fully excavated, but offers some excellent mosaics and monumental public buildings. ⓐ East of Alanya, just west of Anamur town ⏰ Open 08.00–20.00 (summer); 09.00–17.00 (winter) ⓘ Admission charge

Marmure Castle ★★

The remains of Marmure Castle are some of the best on the Turkish coast. Built by the Byzantines and expanded by Alâeddin Keykubad, who built the citadel at Alanya, it has a romantic setting on the water. The crennellated walls saw action up until the beginning of the 20th century and are so authentic that they are often used as a film set for Turkish films. ⓐ East of Anamur ⏰ Open 09.00–17.00 ⓘ Admission charge

Boat Trips to the caverns and Cleopatra's Beach ★★★

The rocky outcrop of the citadel is cut with caverns, particularly on the southern edge bounded by the sea. Many of the small boats in the harbour offer two-, three- or five-hour trips to see the caves. These are at their best in the late afternoons when the sun lights up the insides.

The tour often includes **Phosphorus Cave**, where the water glows an eerie green; **Lover's Cave**, where it is said a German woman and her Turkish boyfriend hid from the police for three months in 1965; **Pirate's Cave**; and **Cleopatra's Beach**, directly under the citadel, where the Egyptian queen came to bathe during her romance with Mark Anthony. ⓐ Alanya Harbour ⓛ Open 09.00–dusk ⓘ Admission charge

The Dimçay River ★

The Dimçay River runs out of the Taurus Mountains to the sea and it is the place to come for freshwater swimming or to enjoy a lunch or dinner of fresh trout, kebabs or *gözleme* at the cafés that line the banks. The tables are set on wooden platforms in the cool river shallows. ⓐ 6 km (4 miles) from the city centre ⓛ Open 24 hours ⓘ Admission free

RESTAURANTS (see map on page 13)

🍴 **Eski Ev €€€ ❶** Meaning 'Old House', this is one of the finest restaurants on this part of the coast. The dining room of the converted mansion is the perfect place to enjoy grand Turkish cuisine, or you can take a table out in the garden. ⓐ Damlataş Caddesi 44 ⓣ 0242 511 6054 ⓛ Open 18.00–23.00

🍴 **Ganzientap Başpinar € ❷** A sure-fire winner for hungry mouths at lunch-time, or in the evening if you want a filling meal before shopping or a bar crawl, Ganzientap Başpinar serves excellent Turkish fast food as well as delicious, slow-cooked stews that you can savour. ⓐ Gazipaşa Caddesi ⓛ Open 11.00–midnight

 Işkele €€€ ❸ Set in the tiny harbour, Işkele is slightly more expensive than its neighbours but the service is a little more

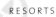
refined and worth it if you want to dress up and make an event of it. The menu concentrates on fish and seafood. 🅐 Işkele Caddesi at Tersane Sokak 🅣 0242 511 0304 🅛 Open 11.00–midnight

Mahperi €€ ❹ A restaurant that has been in business for decades, so you know it is of a good standard. The waterfront setting is lovely. The menu concentrates on fish, but you can also order the less expensive range of kebabs. 🅐 Gazipaşa Caddesi 🅣 0242 512 5491 🅛 Open 11.00–23.00

Ottoman House €€€ ❺ One of the best addresses in Alanya, this restaurant has had a loyal following for years. Set, as the name suggests, in an old Ottoman mansion, it serves good Turkish cuisine, including slow-cooked lamb and *mezes*. You can dine in the garden or on one of the terraces. 🅐 Damlataş Caddesi 31 🅣 0242 511 1421 🅛 Open 17.00–23.00

NIGHTLIFE (see map on page 13)
Bistro Bellman ❻ Bistro Bellman is Alanya's largest open-air disco and its trendiest venue. Close to the harbour, it is set on two tiers and has five bars, several dance floors, and cool terraces with sofas. The DJ concentrates on the latest chart dance tracks and pop. It is also open for dinner (until midnight) and serves Turkish, European and Latin dishes, and has great views over the harbour. 🅐 Işkele Caddesi 4 🅣 0242 512 1992 🅛 Open noon–03.30

James Dean ❼ One of Alanya's largest clubs, the recently renovated James Dean has ten bars set on four different dance floors, with at least two kinds of music on each floor. There is plenty of opportunity to either dance or relax in comfortable sofas and seating areas. They also have guest DJs from Istanbul and Germany. The music is generally a mix of chart, pop, R&B and lounge. 🅐 Işkele Caddesi Rihtim Sokak 32 🅣 0242 513 6101 🅦 www.jamesdeanbaralanya.com 🅛 Open 20.00–04.00

● *Alanya has a good range of bars and restaurants*

Robin Hood ❽ The staff here really do dress up as Robin Hood and his Merry Men, and the decor theme is Sherwood Forest. A fun nightclub with great harbour views from the open-air terraces. Music is chart and pop. ❸ İşkele Caddesi 24 ☎ 0242 512 7923 ◷ Open 21.00–03.00

Antalya
the Mediterranean's cosmopolitan city resort

The anchor city of the Mediterranean coast, Antalya is, aside from Istanbul, the most 'happening' city in Turkey, with a university and new, hi-tech industries attracting a young, energetic and high-earning population. It is the perfect place to capture the 'East meets West' spirit that is modern Turkey.

Set on a wide, sandy bay backed by the ruggedly beautiful Taurus Mountains, Antalya has a wonderful location that has been the focus of many a passing conqueror. It is also in the sunniest part of Turkey, where temperatures stay comfortable throughout the winter – perfect for an early or late trip.

Antalya's tourist attractions act as a magnet for holidaymakers from all along the coast. The old town, Kaleiçi (see page 26), is a large medieval enclave, its cobbled streets and Ottoman mansions dripping with atmosphere, while at its waterside, the Roman harbour is the focal point of boat trips by day, evening strolls and the city's famed nightlife. Further history beckons at the Archaeological Museum (see page 24), which is the best in south-west Turkey.

Despite its size, Antalya has a lively international tourist strip west of the downtown area away from the urban sprawl, taking advantage of the long beach. Here you will find all the water sports and holiday activities you would expect at the newly created and vast Beach Park (see page 24), but the 'buzzing' city is just on your doorstep.

 Antalya tourist office ⓐ Cumhuriyet Caddesi 90
ⓕ 0242 241 1747/4384

HISTORY
The Persians founded Antalya in 158 BC on the site of a deep natural harbour. This was an important port throughout ancient times, and was prized by the Romans and Byzantines because it was safe and

MURAT PASA CAMII

10 ANTALYA BEACH
PARK & AKM

ANKARA,
TERMESSOS
& OTOGAR

FAHRETTIN ALTAY CADDESI

FRIDAY MARKET

MILLI EGEMENLIK CADDASI

KAZIMIZALP CADDESI

ISMET PASA CADDESI

BAZAAR

2

ATATÜRK CADDESI

i

CUMHURIYET CADDASI

YIVLI MINARE
COMPLEX

UZUN CARSI SOKAK

9

PASA CAMIL SOKAK

HIDIRLIK SOKAK

4

HADRIAN'S GATE

ARCHAEOLOGICAL
MUSEUM & KONYAALTI

5

CITY
WALLS

Kalekapisi

11

1

7

CIVELEK SOKAK

HALK PAZARI

Old
Harbour

12 **6**

CITY
WALLS

Kaleiçi

8

HESAPÇI SOKAK

3

CITY
WALLS

Mermerli
Beach

N

0   200 m
0   0.125 mile

13

Mermerli &
Karaalioğlu Parks

IŞIKLAR CADDESI

MEDITERRANEAN
SEA

LARA & DÜDEN
WATERFALLS

23

gave them easy access to the whole Eastern Mediterranean. When the Ottomans took over the city in the 16th century, it was surrounded by a 5 km (3 mile) long wall. They divided it into four districts housing the Greek, Jewish and Muslim communities, and also the ruling classes, or Mamelukes. After the fall of the Ottoman Empire, the harbour was still an important port, but Kaleiçi – the old town within the walls – lost its commercial role and its mansions became dilapidated.

THINGS TO SEE & DO

Antalya Beach Park ★★★

Antalya Beach Park to the west of the downtown core is a pre-planned leisure area with a wide range of children's activities that also suit adults. The two major attractions are: **Aqualand**, a water park with rides, a wave pool, an activity pool with caves to explore, plus an area of 650 sq m (711 sq yd) for children under 6 to play; and **Dolphinland**, with, as you would expect, regular dolphin shows and a 'swim with the dolphins' programme. ➌ Dunlupinar Bulvari, Konyaaltı Korulugu Yani ➊ 0242 249 0900 Ⓦ www.beachpark.com.tr

Antalya Archaeological Museum ★★★

This is one of the best archaeological museums of ancient finds in the Eastern Mediterranean, with artefacts from sites all around the region. The main collections worth viewing – many of them are given their own rooms – are as follows:

Finds from Perge The highlight of the museum is the collection of artefacts from the ancient city of Perge to the east of Antalya (see Excursions, page 56). The highly decorated monumental statuary (mostly 2nd century AD) shows how sophisticated the city must have been in its heyday. The collection of ornamental friezes that decorated the theatre at Perge are to be considered the finest of their kind in the world.

◆ *Dolphinland provides regular shows for families*

Byzantine and Christian items The prize item here is the reliquary that is said to have held the bones of the 4th-century Bishop of Myra, St Nicholas, or Baba Noel, as he is known in Turkish, the saint on whom the modern legend of Santa Claus is based (see Excursions, page 71)

Bronze Age finds Items here date from the 6th to the 8th century BC, when the Phrygian people inhabited the area. Keep an eye out for the exquisite statuary and funerary urns. There are also finds from the Karain Cave – the earliest populated site yet found in Turkey (see page 64).

Ethnological Collection This room holds a fine collection of Selçuk and Ottoman handicrafts, with a diorama of a traditional nomadic lifestyle showing how many Turks lived until the 20th century (and, in fact, how some still do). ⓐ Cumhuriyet Caddesi ⓛ Open Tues–Sun 09.00–18.00, closed Mon ⓘ Admission charge

Atatürk Kültür Merkezi (or AKM) ★

This huge exhibition complex – a copy of the Louvre pyramid in Paris – is the basis of Antalya's cultural life, hosting the International Film Festival and regular plays and concerts, with everything from pop to the Antalya Symphony Orchestra. With its lovely parkland, this is the place to come for a stroll or to take tea at one of the cafés. ➌ 100 Yil Bulvari ☏ 0242 244 0328 🕒 Open 10.00–18.00 and in the evenings for performances

Kaleiçi ★★★

This labyrinth of narrow alleyways and courtyarded mansions is still evocative of Ottoman Turkey, although today the quarter is home to stylish boutique hotels, upmarket restaurants and bohemian shops. There is no set route, just follow your nose around the next picture-perfect corner, browsing as you go. You will be able to explore excellent renovations or evocative ruins, but whether the mansion is a palace or the pits, the beauty is in the detail – wooden lintels, stone archways and a palate of weather-worn pastel stucco walls add to the atmosphere.

City Walls ★★

Various sections of the old city walls survive. At the main entrance to Kaleiçi, Kalekapısı, a section of wall, supports Saat Kulesi, a Seljuk clock tower. Other sections run from the harbour around the rocky coastline, but the longest and most impressive stretch runs south of Hadrian's Gate.

Yivli Minare (Fluted Minaret) ★★

Built in 1230 by Sultan Alâeddin Keykubad, Yivli Minare, so called because the minaret has a fluted tower, has become a symbol of Antalya. The mosque next door is still used for worship.

Hadrian's Gate ★★

This is one of the best preserved monuments in Antalya. Built on the eastern flank of Roman Antalya in AD 130, this triumphal arch celebrated a visit to the city by Emperor Hadrian. A flight of steps leading down to the gate shows just how much higher the modern city is than the one that existed in Roman times.

Old Harbour ★ ★ ★

Down on the shore below the mansions of Kaleiçi, the harbour is now a pleasure marina with a flotilla of little boats offering tours of the bay. There are several cafés and restaurants, so it is a popular place for an early evening drink or dinner. While you are relaxing you can examine the walls of the harbour, which were built by the Romans, although they have been reinforced regularly since then, and watch young and old out for a stroll in the cooler evening air.

Mermerli and Karaalioğlu Parks ★

A welcome place to relax under the shade, the parks offer tea rooms and play areas for children. Think of this as somewhere to cool off after your tour of the old town.

Turkish baths & spas ★

For a relaxing break from sightseeing and sunbathing, try a turkish bath or spa.

Nazır Hammam This Turkish bath has mixed sessions in the evenings.
ⓐ Hammam Aralığı Sokak (behind Mehmet Paşa Mosque)
🕒 Open 07.00–20.00

Serenity Spa This is a well-equipped spa with mud-chamber massages, exfoliations and body treatments. There is also a traditional *hammam*, jacuzzi and sauna. ⓐ Sheraton Voyager Hotel 100 Yil Bulvari
🕿 0242 238 5555 Ⓦ www.starwoodhotels.com

Diving ★

Rainbow Dive Centre This popular centre offers dive training and guided diving for qualified divers. ⓐ Yat Limani (in the old harbour)
🕿 0242 248 1257

SHOPPING

Antalya is famous throughout Turkey for its jams and preserves. **Halk Pazarı**, or People's Market, does a great line in designer fakes, but is also the permanent fruit and vegetable market for the city. Or try **Pazar**, which has the usual range of Turkish souvenirs and also a refurbished traditional gold market, **Iki Kapılar Hanı**. There are some great shopping venues in Kaleiçi, often renovated mansions housing bohemian boutiques and carpet shops. This is the place to buy an unusual item rather than mass-produced souvenirs. The atmosphere is a little less frenetic than in the tourist bazaars and prices are generally higher.

Antalya has some excellent modern shops that cater directly to its young affluent urbanites. A wander along Atatürk Caddesi and Işıklar Caddesi is as exciting as any high street back home and a little more glitzy than most.

The **Migros Shopping Centre** on Bulvari Arapsuyu Mevkii is one of a new breed of American-style shopping malls with a huge hypermarket, 96 shops and an entertainment centre.

The 'duty-free zone' next to the modern port west of the city also has a modern mall-style shopping area.

BEACHES

Konyaaltı is a long, wide bay stretching out west of the city centre along the shoreline of the Gulf of Antalya. Konyaalti now fronts Antalya's expanding 'hotel district'. The whole section is actually split into 12 differently named pebble beach areas, each with its own access, cafés and activities, which range from water sports to beach volleyball and soccer. The attractions of the **Antalya Beach Park** (see page 24) are also just on hand. There is a shelf just offshore here, so make sure you keep young children and non-swimmers to the shallows. To the east of town, beach activities tend to centre on several private beach clubs (❶ Entrance fee) with no sand but artificial lidos. They are not ideal for younger children, but perfect for those who do not like getting sand mixed with their sun lotion. The closest one to the city is the **Adalar Club**, which you can reach from Karaalioglu Park. **Mermerli** beach is another small stretch of sand and pebbles south-east of the harbour wall.

EXCURSIONS
Boat trips ★★★
Head to the old harbour, where a flotilla of boats offers tours out into the Gulf of Antalya or to the beach at Konyaaltı. A popular destination is the lower Düden Falls (see below).

Düden Falls ★
A lovely area of several cascades surrounded by some lovely verdant landscapes, the Düden Falls make a perfect excursion from the city. The lower Düden Falls are the most impressive, dropping 30 m (98 ft) directly into the Mediterranean. A crowd of tour boats visits every day from all around the Gulf of Antalya to watch the spectacle.

To visit the upper falls 9 km (6 miles) inland you can take a dolmuş or rent a car. The multiple cascades are surrounded by verdant woodland with lots of places to enjoy a picnic and tea gardens for refreshment. You can walk directly behind the cascade, which is a thrilling experience.

The falls are always busy on summer weekends when families from Antalya visit for an afternoon of relaxation. ⓐ 15 km (9 miles) north of Antalya ◷ Open 08.00–sunset ❶ Admission charge

RESTAURANTS (see map on page 23)
🍴 **Anfi** €€ ❶ In the harbour, this is a really popular restaurant with locals because it serves excellent food at reasonable prices. Try the *meze* dishes. There is also a large terrace with views across the harbour to the citadel. ⓐ Kaleici Yat Limani (in the old port) ❶ 0242 243 2073

Dönerciler Çarşısı (Döner Market) € **2** This popular area has lots of cheap *döner* and *pide* stalls and as a result has become known as the '*döner* market'. It is a place for young Turks to hang out and meet their girlfriends and boyfriends. No stall really stands out, but it is a great place to stop for a quick, cheap lunch during your sightseeing trip. ⓐ Corner of Cumhuriyet and Atatürk Caddesi 🕐 Open 08.00–01.00

Gül €€ **3** A Turkish/German-owned restaurant frequented by locals and resident ex-pats. Offers a good range of traditional dishes that are well cooked and not overpriced, and you can relax in the garden for a pleasant lunch or dinner. ⓐ Kocatepe Sokak 1 ☎ 0242 247 5126 🕐 Open 11.00–midnight

Hasanağa €€ **4** Popular with locals thanks to the live Turkish music every night. The *mezes* are fantastic. Try them together with *raki* for a truly Turkish meal. The atmosphere is very authentic. ⓐ Mescit Sokak 15 ☎ 0242 242 8105 🕐 Open 11.00–01.00

Hisar Teşişleri €€ **5** This restaurant is set in the ramparts of the old town, and has a terrace overlooking the bay. You therefore come here as much for the views as for the food – both of which are excellent. ⓐ Cumhuriyet Meydani Kaleiçi ☎ 0242 241 5281 🕐 Open 11.00–16.00 and 18.00–midnight

Kirkmerdivan (40 Steps) €€€ **6** The menu concentrates on meat grills, either typically Turkish or European in style, with various sauces. Eat in the air-conditioned dining room or out on the shady terrace. Either way, the Ottoman music accompanying your meal will be a pleasant change from the latest Euro pop. ⓐ Mermerli Sokak, Selçuk Mah ☎ 0242 242 9686 🕐 Open 11.00–midnight

Sirri Restaurant €€–€€€ **7** The beautiful Ottoman decor of this renovated mansion with its verdant garden sets the scene for your meal in this restaurant. The menu concentrates on fresh fish

and typical dishes like delicious *guveç*. ⓐ Uzun Çarşi Sokak 25
ⓣ 0242 241 7239 ⓛ Open 11.00–midnight

Villa Perla €€–€€€ ⑧ A beautiful converted mansion, and
now a boutique hotel with a highly regarded restaurant. Tables
are set around the atmospheric and flower-strewn courtyard. There
is an international clientele. Turkish and Continental cuisine. ⓐ Hesapçı
Sokak 26 ⓣ 0242 248 9793 ⓛ Open 11.00–15.00 and 18.00–23.00

NIGHTLIFE (see map on page 23)
Ali Baba Rock Café ⑨ Modelled on the other famous rock cafés but
without the memorabilia, the music is live and loud with mostly local
offerings. ⓐ Uzun Çarşi Sokak 24 ⓣ 0242 243 4937 ⓛ Open 16.00-03.00

Discoland ⑩ Set within the Aqualand waterpark complex, it is fun and
has music and lots of water, so something a bit different. ⓐ Dumlupinar
Bulvari, Konyaaltı Korulugu Yani ⓣ 0242 249 0900 ⓛ Open 22.00–03.00
(summer); Thurs–Sun 22.00-03.00 (winter)

Disco Alli (Ally) ⑪ Open-air disco that is the place to be in the city, with
foam parties, laser shows and eight bars. It sprawls across land around
the Roman walls in the old part of town. ⓐ Selçuk Mah, Musalla Sokak,
Kaleiçi ⓣ 0242 244 3000 ⓛ Open 22.00–04.00

Kale Bar ⑫ Overlooking the harbour, this bar is the perfect place in
Antalya for an after-dinner drink and to watch the 'promenaders' by
the water's edge. ⓐ Mermerli Banyo Sokak 2 ⓣ 0242 248 6478
ⓛ Open 11.00–03.00

North Shield ⑬ The nearest thing that Antalya has to an English
pub, the North Shield is a restored mansion that sells imported beers
and is really popular with the young and trendy Antalya crowd. It has
a nice setting in the parkland. ⓐ Karaalioğlu Park ⓣ 0242 330 3030
ⓛ Open 11.00–03.00

N

| 0 | 200 m |
| 0 | 0.125 mile |

Western
Beach

MANAVGAT

SORGUN YOLU

MEDITERRANEAN
SEA

ANCIENT
CITY WALLS

SIDE
MUSEUM

VESPASIAN
ARCH/CITY GATE

AGORA

BYZANTINE
BASILICA

ANCIENT
THEATRE

TURGUTREIS SOKAK

CAMI SOKAK

4

7 1

LIMANI CADDESI

3

6

Harbour

5

2

Eastern
Beach

TEMPLES OF
APOLLO & ATHENA

Side
where ancient meets modern

Side (pronounced See-day) means 'pomegranate' in an ancient Anatolian dialect – although no one is really sure why this was used as a place name. Today, Side is unique along the Turkish Coast; an ancient site wrapped in a modern, bustling holiday resort.

The compact town centre sits on a rocky promontory that is closed to traffic in the evenings. It is an atmospheric mix of shops, restaurants and bars that is perfect for a simple stroll or some serious bar crawling. Either side of the promontory, the long, sandy beaches are great for bronzing and water sports. The western side of town is most developed, with a ribbon of hotels backing the strand. From here it is a stroll along the beachside promenade into the heart of Side.

Side combines everything that is good about a holiday in Turkey – some great ancient history that is not too overwhelming, good beaches and cheeky banter from the shopkeepers who sell the whole range of Turkish souvenirs, plus great nightlife from chic bars to noisy nightclubs.

HISTORY
Side was one of the major slave markets in the area from soon after it was founded in the 7th century BC. Sacked by Arab forces in the 7th century AD, it was still occupied in the 11th century but was then abandoned, perhaps after earthquake damage. The site was not resettled until the 1920s, by Muslim fishermen from Crete who came after the exchange of populations between Greeks and Turks. It remained a quiet fishing port until the arrival of tourism.

THINGS TO SEE & DO
Agora ★
This was the site of the main slave market in the Greek era, but the most interesting building here is the remains of a Roman, 24-seat communal latrine – people were not as shy in those days as they are now!

Ancient road ★★

Situated between the baths and the *agora* (and on the modern approach road into town after the tourist office), there are interesting sections of the ancient colonnaded road that was the main access to the town.

Ancient theatre ★★★

Where most of Turkey's ancient amphitheatres are built into hillsides, Side's is totally free-standing and makes a very impressive sight. Built by the Greeks, it was expanded by the Romans to seat 15,000. The interior has an interesting feature – a wall around the orchestra, built to protect audiences from the wild animals used in gladiatorial contests and to allow the orchestra to be flooded to hold mock naval battles.
ⓐ At the entrance to the modern town ⓒ Open 08.00–22.00
ⓘ Admission charge

Byzantine Basilica ★

Surrounding the site of the temples of Apollo and Athena (see opposite) are the remains of a large early Christian basilica with some wonderful Romanesque architecture such as columns and small, arched windows. Part of the site has been taken over by bars and cafés, offering some of the most romantic and atmospheric settings in Side for a pre- or post-dinner drink.

City walls ★★

Sections of the Roman city walls run down each side of the promontory and across the landward approaches. Some are free-standing, but others are now disguised by more modern architecture. It is always worth keeping a lookout for the walls as you stroll around the town.

Roman Baths ★★

The well-preserved Roman Baths have been converted into the Side Museum and they now display a selection of fine statuary discovered at the site, and hundreds of pieces of decorative friezes and bits of stonework that really bring to life how attractive the city must have

looked a couple of thousand years ago. ❸ Side Museum, in town centre
🕐 Open 08.00–noon and 13.00–17.00 (summer); Tues-Sun same hours
(winter) ❶ Admission charge

Side Harbour ★★

A tiny harbour, with stone outcrops (ancient artificial breakwaters) at
either side that give the Side promontory the look of a crab with its
claws out, is the home of some lovely wooden tour boats and the odd
fishing vessel. It is the place for an evening stroll, and is lined with bars
and restaurants ranging from basic eateries to relatively exclusive,
upmarket places. Prices are more expensive than in the town streets,
but you pay for the views.

Temples of Apollo and Athena ★★

Set in a lovely position just by the water, these two 2nd-century AD
temples make an atmospheric place to come and watch the sun set.

⬤ *The Temple of Apollo at sunset*

Some of the stonework has been re-erected to form an arch decorated with extremely fine carved detail.

Vespasian Arch and City Gate ★★
This marks the entrance into the town even in modern times. It has a fine, carved pediment on top of its Corinthian columns.

Water parks ★★
Waterplanet With 23 slides and rides, a 350 m (383 yd) artificial river for rafting, wave pools, bars, restaurants and a disco, this is a well-thought-out water park with something for the whole family. @ Okurcalar Mevkii, Manavgat ❶ 0242 527 5164 ⓦ www.waterplanet.com.tr ❶ Open 08.00–18.00 (closing times vary with season) ❶ Admission charge
Club Ali Bey Manavgat Aquapark Part of a holiday village complex, with a range of pools, rides and slides. @ Manavgat Alanya Karayolu, Manavgat ❶ 0242 748 7373 ⓦ www.clubalibeymanavgat.com.tr ❶ Open 08.00–18.00 (closing times vary with season) ❶ Admission charge

BEACHES
The rocky promontory where you find the town centre is flanked by good beaches. West of the town there is a long, slender beach reaching for several kilometres around the bay, and this is where the hotels and apartments were built in the 1970s and 1980s. The eastern beaches are wider and until the 1990s were totally unspoilt. Several larger hotel complexes offering generally more upmarket accommodation have been built recently. There is also a small, rocky beach on the south side of the promontory off Barbarosa Caddesi. For beaches further afield, take a dolmuş to **Sorgun** (3 km/2 miles east) and **Kumköy** (10 km/6 miles west).

EXCURSIONS
Manavgat Şelale (Manavgat Waterfalls) ★★
Niagara Falls they are not, but these tumbling, picturesque cataracts surrounded by verdant gardens make a refreshing trip from the sometimes stifling coastal strip.

SHOPPING

Barriers at the upper end of town limit traffic, and the main pedestrian streets of the downtown core offer some of the best and most typical tourist shopping in the region – it is to all intents and purposes a bazaar, but with shops rather than stalls. You will find everything here from gold to leather to carpets, plus the usual piles of T-shirts and socks. It is a very atmospheric place, especially in the evenings.

A line of simpler stalls selling pottery, cheap jewellery and other budget items stretches out around the bay on the West Beach boardwalk.

Several sets of horseshoe falls – the highest of these has a 3 m (10 ft) drop – cleanse the air with cooling water vapour and there is a large café/tourist site nearby for refreshments and (mostly) tacky souvenirs.

The boat trip up the Manavgat River from Side (or the shorter trip from the town of Manavgat) is a lovely way to spend a day just watching the river banks pass by.

Weekends are often very busy as the falls are a popular picnic site for Turkish families from the surrounding area.

Alarahan ★ ★ ★
It is worth the trip to see this town with its nearby ruins (see page 17).

Boat trips ★
The most popular boat trip from Side is to the waterfalls at Manavgat (see above).

If you have your own transport, head upriver from the falls. You can lose the crowds and there are some lovely shady cafés or riverside picnic sites where you can spend time playing in the fresh water.

● *Shop at the atmospheric stalls in Side*

RESTAURANTS (see map on page 32)

🍴 **Aphrodite** €€–€€€ ❶ This restaurant on the main square has been here a while so it must be reliable, although it is a bit more expensive than its neighbours. The menu has the usual meats and fish, plus a special fish stew cooked in a clay pot that needs to be pre-ordered. ⓐ Liman Caddesi ❶ 0242 753 1171 ❶ Open 08.00–midnight

🍴 **Moonlight** €€ ❷ As the name suggests, this is an open-air restaurant, where you eat by candlelight on the water's edge – perfect for a romantic meal for two. The menu has fish and a range of European dishes, including some vegetarian options. ⓐ Barbaros Caddesi 49 ❶ 0242 753 1400 ❶ Open 11.00–01.00

🍴 **Ottoman Restaurant** €€ ❸ The best value on the harbour – this restaurant still attracts local clientele, which is always a good sign. The Ottoman serves Turkish cuisine and seafood, so come and try something a little different. ❸ Liman Caddesi ☎ 0242 753 1434 🕒 Open 11.00–01.00

🍴 **Soundwaves** €€ ❹ You will find good value meals at this quiet restaurant, which concentrates on seafood with several flambéed specialities. ❸ At the west end of Eastern Beach

NIGHTLIFE (see map on page 32)
The Blues Bar ❺ A bar with great live music and the usual lively bar atmosphere. ❸ Camii Sokak ☎ 0242 753 1197 🕒 Open 19.00–03.00

Kiss Bar ❻ A busy bar that acts as a popular meeting place to start or end the evening. ❸ Barbaros Caddesi 23 ☎ 0242 753 3482 🕒 Open 16.00–03.00

Lighthouse ❼ This unusual setting for a bar fires out high-energy music right across the town every night. ❸ Liman Caddesi, on the northern side of the promontory by the harbour ☎ 0242 753 3588 🕒 Open 22.00–03.00

Oxyd ❽ The place to be on this part of the coast, it is a massive open-air place with a capacity of 3,000 and several different-style areas, including a swimming pool. You can get transport out there but it is a taxi ride back. ❸ Denizbuku Mevkii, 3 km (2 miles) west of the town centre on Western Beach ☎ 0242 753 4940 🌐 www.disco-oxyd.com 🕒 Open 22.00–04.00

↘ If you have a rental car, do not park it on the approach to the town, because it will be towed away. Use the large and inexpensive car park just before the pedestrian area.

🔺 *Moonlight Park Beach – one of the fine stretches of sandy beach at Kemer*

Kemer, Beldibi & Tekirova
the Mediterranean's marina resort

Kemer is one of the earliest government-approved and therefore carefully planned tourist developments to have sprung up along the Turkish coast since the late 1980s. This narrow corridor of the land south-west of Antalya had never had a large natural population, but was ripe for tourist development. A great beach, pristine waters and a magnificent backdrop of pine-clad rocky peaks were the idyllic natural stage on which to build a resort.

The resort itself, however, is not one of the most picturesque places – lots of functional, white-painted concrete – but what Kemer lacks in charm it makes up for in facilities, including an upmarket marina that attracts a wealthy international clientele.

Everything for a fun beach holiday is here, plus classy shopping – although the nightlife is a little more laid back than further east along the coast. Over time, development has expanded along the coast with other small resorts at Beldibi and Tekirova. These have a predominance of large, all-inclusive resort hotels, and Kemer is the lively heart of the 'strip'.

HISTORY

Kemer was the site of the ancient city of Idyros, or Likya, but nothing of this remains and little is known about it. By the early 20th century there was only a simple village on the site, but it suffered flooding from rain from the Olymbos Mountains. To counteract this, the local people built over 20 km (12 miles) of walls to protect the village. Kemer means 'belt' in Turkish – the name comes from these protective structures.

THINGS TO SEE & DO

Kemer Marina ★★

This is one of the finest modern marinas along the Turkish coast, with berths for 300 yachts and other boats. There are some fantastic and extremely expensive craft here and it's the perfect place to enjoy the maritime atmosphere and watch the activities of the crews and clients.

Moonlight Park Beach ★★★

Most of what Kemer has to offer in terms of what to do happens here. The long, sandy beach is a major draw, but add to this some good activities and a collection of restaurants, cafés and shops, and you have somewhere you can spend the whole day. The following sections are certainly worth a visit:

Mini-Club A programme specially designed for youngsters where they get to play games and enjoy arts and crafts, so parents can leave them knowing they are fully supervised.

Swimming pool A large, freshwater pool for those who do not want to swim in the sea.

Amphitheatre A 500-capacity, traditionally styled open-air venue that hosts cultural shows during the day and converts into a cinema in the evenings – this generally shows international films, but with Turkish subtitles.

Dolphinarium Undoubtedly the highlight of a visit to Moonlight Park, the three bottlenose dolphins and a huge sea lion perform three shows a day for a capacity 800 audience. You can also 'swim with the dolphins', spending some time in the pool.

Natureland ★★★

This offbeat theme park (and hotel accommodation) is unique in Turkey,
and also offers thalassotherapy treatments and a traditional Chinese
wellness centre with massage, acupuncture and medicinal treatments.
Its main highlights are:

Aquarium Park This is a combined aquarium and water park where
you can watch the sea life of the Mediterranean in its salt-water home
(the first of its kind in Turkey), and then enjoy an hour or so having fun
on the water slides and in the freshwater pools, take diving lessons or
simply enjoy the beach with its water sports.

Country Park An ecological and folkloric reserve where the organic
farming practices of old rural Turkey have been rekindled. You can
eat food made with the crops grown here, at the cafés on site. There
are also colourful parades, magic shows and circus acts throughout
the day.

Forest Park Here you can learn all about the forest ecosystem. It is
a fun approach, with parks for youngsters and interactive activities
for older children and adults. There is also a life-size recreation of Noah's
Ark with models of the animals. ⓐ Çamyuva, Kemer ❶ 0242 824 6214
ⓦ www.natureland.com.tr ⓛ Open from 08.00 (closing times vary with
season) ❶ Admission charge

Rally ★

Kemer and the region of the Olymbos Mountains behind the resort
play host to the car-racing event **WRC Rally of Turkey**. Usually held in
early March, the rally had a slot in June in 2005. It is worth checking
to see if it is coming back around to the area in future years.
ⓦ www.wrc.com

Yörük Parki (Nomad Park) ★★

This themed parkland area recreates the traditional lifestyle of the
nomadic Anatolian Turks, and you can enjoy fresh *gözleme* made by
the ladies while the traditionally dressed men serve *ayran* yoghurt

drinks to wash it down. It is a wonderfully cool and relaxing place to visit after a day of bronzing on the beach.

BEACHES

Kemer has many fine stretches of beach – the image of the golden strand backed by verdant heady pine forest is perfectly true here – but most of the coves have pebbles rather than sand. The most sandy beaches are found at **Moonlight Park**, in front of **Yörük Parki** and next to the **marina**.

Diving ★

Aksuna Sports There is some good diving just offshore and this company has a good reputation and operates from the marina. They also have other activities. ❸ H/O Arapsoyu Mevkii, Ebr Apt D3, Antalya ❶ 0242 814 5132 Ⓦ www.aksuna-sports.com

Horse riding ★

Hotel Berkeranch This equestrian centre is also a hotel and offers one- and two-week packages with daily rides, but you can also book lessons or head out on a trail for from one to several hours. There are 26 horses and the complex covers 18 ha (45 acres) of forest. ❸ Akçasaz Mevkii, Çamyuva ❶ 0242 446 0333 Ⓦ www.hotel-berkeranch.com

Turkiz Hotel Thalasso Centre ★

This hotel's large thalassotherapy spa offers a luxurious variety of treatments, including endermology, pressotherapy and seaweed therapy, plus numerous seawater programmes. There is also a *hammam*, steam room, sauna and fitness centre. ❸ Yaki Caddesi 3 ❶ 0242 814 4180 Ⓦ www.turkiz.com.tr

EXCURSIONS

Boat trips ★★★

Several boat trips from the main marina head out to **Olymbos Beach** (see page 74) and to **Phaselis** (see page 45).

◆ *Remains of the fine ampitheatre at Phaselis*

Phaselis ★★
Founded by Greek colonists from Rhodes in the 6th century BC, Phaselis was a major port and trading city for several hundred years. Today the ruins of the city lie among heady pine forest and are interspersed with pretty sandy coves, some of which used to be the old city harbours. You can do a little exploring in between sunbathing, snorkelling and swimming. Under the water you can explore the walls of the old port – now a home for fish and the odd small octopus.

Boat trips along the coast drop you at the site, or there is road access with a ticket office and a small museum and refreshment kiosk – but taking a picnic is better. Note that Phaselis gets very busy at weekends, with families coming here from Antalya, so for a quieter time, visit during the week. ⓐ 15 km (9 miles) south of Kemer ⓛ Open 08.00–19.00 (summer); 08.00–17.30 (winter) ⓘ Admission charge

RESTAURANTS & BARS
Nightlife in the region tends to revolve around the hotel discos and most of the large complexes have one – music tends to be in the bland, Euro-pop style.

Aura A large, open-air club with laser and light shows that is the heart of after-midnight action in the resort. Regular theme nights and foam parties add to the fun. ⓐ Deniz Caddesi 3, Moonlight Park ⓣ 0242 814 5266 ⓛ Open 22.00–03.00 (summer)

Monte Kemer €€€ Favoured restaurant of the World Rally teams when they are in town, Monte Kemer does great steaks. ⓐ Atatürk Caddesi 41 ⓣ 0242 814 6226 ⓛ Open 11.00–midnight

Navigator Bar This bar is the focal point for the yachting crowd. With many ex-pats living on board their boats throughout the year, it is busy throughout the seasons. Great atmosphere with wonderful views across the hundreds of masts. ⓐ Yat Limani, in the marina ⓣ 0242 814 1490 ⓛ Open 08.00–01.00

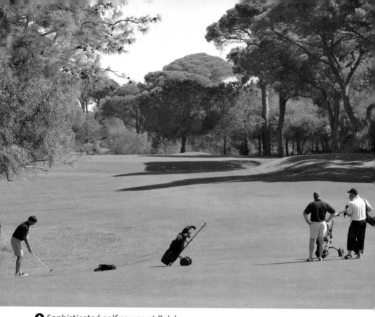

Sophisticated golf course at Belek

Belek
golf capital of the eastern Mediterranean

With over 300 days of sunshine each year and temperatures that rarely drop below 10°C, this sheltered corner of the Mediterranean coast was chosen in the mid-1980s as the site of a new, purpose-planned resort. This was a new concept for Turkish tourism – huge 4- and 5-star hotel complexes offering full board or all-inclusive packages with a high level of service and a whole range of activities on site.

It has been a huge success, and Belek has quickly gained a reputation in the marketplace as a great all-year-active resort. The sporting facilities here attract the main Turkish football teams, Galatasary and Fenerbaçhe, for pre-season training, along with an increasing number of European

teams including Belgium's FC Brugge, Young Boys of Switzerland and
Werder Bremen of Germany.

Belek started on a green-field site, so there is not much authentic
Turkish atmosphere in the resort itself, but it has easy access to Antalya
and other towns and villages along the coast.

THINGS TO SEE & DO
Golf ★★★

Antalya Golf Club Opened in 2003, Antalya Golf Club has state-of-
the-art facilities and a particularly good golf school, with special
provision for junior players. There are two courses here, the par-71, 6411 m
(7013 yd) **Sultan** and the par-72, 5731 m (6270 yd) **Pasha**, both designed
by European Golf Design and consultant David Jones. ➌ Uçkum Tetesi
Mevkii, Serik ➊ 0242 725 5970 Ⓦ www.antalyagolfclub.com.tr

Gloria Golf Resort Opened in 1997, this 18-hole, par-72, 6296 m
(6888 yd) course was designed around several lakes and runs through
pine forest and along the shoreline of the 5-star full-service Gloria
Resort Hotel. A 9-hole course was added in 2001. ➌ Açisu Mevkii
➊ 0242 715 1520 Ⓦ www.gloriagolf.com

National Golf Club This par-72, 6232 m (6818 yd) course was designed
by professional golfer David Feherty and was the first to be opened here
in 1994. It has held several international tournaments and was voted the
world's number 42 course by *Golf World Magazine* in 2001. There is also
a 9-hole, par-29 course, and 40 driving ranges. ➌ Serik ➊ 0242 724 4620
Ⓦ www.nationalturkey.com

Robinson Club Nobilis The largest and most upmarket resort in Belek,
the Nobilis has an excellent range of sporting facilities set around its
upmarket villas and holiday club accommodation. They have a golf
academy staffed by PGA-qualified professionals. The course, designed
by Dave Thomas, borders the Acısu River and makes the most of the
natural terrain. ➌ Açisu Mevkii ➊ 0242 715 1491 Ⓦ www.nobilis.com.tr

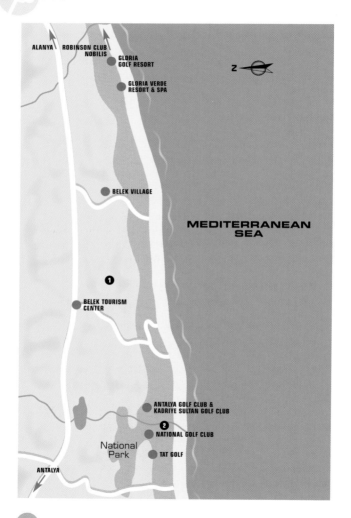

ALANYA   ROBINSON CLUB
NOBILIS

GLORIA
GOLF RESORT

GLORIA VERDE
RESORT & SPA

N

BELEK VILLAGE

MEDITERRANEAN
SEA

❶

BELEK TOURISM
CENTER

ANTALYA GOLF CLUB &
KADRIYE SULTAN GOLF CLUB

❷ NATIONAL GOLF CLUB

National
Park   TAT GOLF

ANTALYA

Tat Golf – International Golf Club

Tat features three separate 9-hole courses that can be combined to an 18- or 27-hole round. The Tat, Belek and International 9s each have a par of 36 with a length of around 3200 m (3500 yd). ❷ Uçkum Tepesi Mevkii ❶ 0242 725 5303 ❿ www.tatbeach.com

Water Sports ★

Belek caters to all kinds of water sports – whatever you are looking for, it is likely to be on offer for you. Most of the major hotels run their own water-sports rental and instruction centres. These are also open to non-residents.

Spas ★

The Robinson Club Nobilis Offers a full package of well-being programmes, be it diet, fitness, meditation or body therapies. They have licensed trainers as well as systematically designed programmes, and a bistro that will prepare meals tailored to your programme (see page 47 for contact details).

Gloria Verde Resort & Spa The thalassotherapy spa here specializes in 'thalgo' treatments using plant extracts imported from France in conjunction with sea-water therapies. They also have a full range of massage and wellness treatments (see page 47 for contact details).

BEACHES

Belek sits on the western stretch of a fine, sandy beach that runs all around the bay to Antalya (30 km/19 miles away). The beach has a shallow draft and is especially suitable for families and for bathing. Walk away from the main resorts in either direction and you can find a quieter spot, but without sunbed rental and sun umbrellas.

EXCURSIONS

Zeytintaşi Cave ★

Discovered by accident in 1997, Zeytintaşi is a massive two-level cave some 14 m (46 ft) below ground with exceptional columns, stalactites and stalagmites. It is famed for its 'macaroni' stalactites – long, thin strands of hardened calcium that hang from the cave roof. **ⓐ** 28 km (17 miles) inland, near Serik **ⓛ** Open 09.00–18.00 **ⓘ** Admission charge

Birdwatching ★

Data collected to date has revealed that of approximately 450 bird species known in Turkey today, 109 are found in this region. Certain of these species are on the verge of extinction or highly endangered. Of particular recent interest was biologists' breeding of the endangered *Tyto alba* (hooded owl). **Ezop Travel** (based in Istanbul) offer birdwatching trips. **ⓦ** www.ezoptravel.com

Turtle spotting ★★

The beaches around Belek are a favoured nesting spot for turtles (*Caretta caretta*), and most hotels offer guided walks.

RESTAURANTS (see map on page 48)

Roman Bar and Restaurant €€ **❶** This is the one place in the resort where you can sit down with a cold beer and watch Sky Sports, or enjoy an evening of karaoke with your friends. The place to come if you're looking for the English crowd. **ⓐ** Cumhuriyet Caddesi N8/c, Kadriye Beldesi **ⓣ** 0242 725 5363 **ⓛ** Open 10.00–03.00

The Park Café €–€€ **❷** Overlooking the lake and the 18th hole of the National Golf Course, the Park Café is a relaxing place for a late breakfast, lunch or afternoon snack. The menu offers international light meals and snacks, but also a delicious selection of traditional Turkish food, including *gözleme* cooked as you watch. **ⓐ** Serik **ⓣ** 0242 724 4620 **ⓦ** www.nationalturkey.com **ⓛ** Open 11.00–17.00

EXCURSIONS
Out & about

Around the Mediterranean

THINGS TO SEE & DO

A Turkish evening ★ ★ ★

Genuine Turkish food and entertainment may be difficult to find in many modern resorts, but the 'Turkish evening' offers the perfect introduction to the culture. You will start with a buffet meal of *meze* dishes, barbecued meats and salads washed down with local wine or beer, after which you will be entertained by folkloric dances, plus of course the famous 'belly dance'. Someone from the audience is always invited to have a go, which is generally amusing for everyone watching. Later in the evening the dance floor is handed over to the guests for an hour or so of disco dancing.

Gület cruise ★ ★ ★

It's really not a true Turkish holiday if you don't get out onto the water. From offshore you can really appreciate the beauty of the landscape, the verdant pine forests, olive groves and unspoilt beaches and coves. You may even be lucky enough to spot a dolphin or a turtle.

The traditional Turkish wooden boat is one of the most beautiful and distinctive craft in the Mediterranean and you will find them in all Turkish ports. You can rent them privately, but why bother – there's a vast choice of day trips available for very reasonable prices. You can enjoy lunch and take a swim before returning to your resort at about 17.00 or 18.00 in time to shower and change for your evening meal.

Jeep or 4x4 safari ★ ★ ★

The jeep safari is a real adventure. Out and about on roads you would probably never find yourself in a rental car, it gives you a chance to see the traditional Turkish way of life and discover the countryside around your resort. The day includes a traditional lunch and a spot of shopping at a craft market or carpet warehouse. Routes vary, but here are two:

Western Lycian peaks From Kemer and the west there are exciting routes into the western Lycian peaks behind the resort, with high mountain scenery along roads that traverse the mountain ridges. Routes from Antalya can follow the same roads, or head north into the Taurus Mountains where the coastal plain meets the Anatolian land-mass. The Köprülü Valley (see page 62) is a popular site.

Around Side & Alanya The coastal plain is much wider at Side, so the scenery is less dramatic than in the west of the region, but there are compensations because there are far more rural communities here, plus a couple of good carpet cooperatives where you can see traditional methods of

⬥ *Belly dancing at a Turkish evening*

silk and wool production, natural dying and weaving. Alanya may share some of the same routes as Side, or you may head into the hills to the *yaylas*, or summer resorts, where the Ottomans would come to spend time in the cooler air away from the oppressive heat of the coast.

Village tours ★★
Most Mediterranean resorts have lost their traditional ways of life as tourism has developed, so a village tour is the perfect way to see how the vast majority of Turks away from the cities and the coastal strip live. The Taurus Mountains running inland from the Mediterranean coast have some wonderful rural settlements where life continues almost as it has done for the last few hundred years – with the rhythm of the seasons. Worth a visit to see a different way of life.

Turkish Baths ★ ★ ★

Not only will you be squeaky clean and relaxed, but your suntan will last far longer. What better reason to try a traditional Turkish bath, or as the locals call it, a *hammam*?

History Cleanliness is very important in Islamic cultures, where face, hands and feet must be clean before each prayer session. The communal *hammams* were a place where hot water could be guaranteed and where men or women could come and have a good gossip. During Ottoman times it was grounds for divorce if a man refused his wife bath money. Today, although many town houses and apartments have all the mod cons, it is still a popular social activity.

What to expect Traditional *hammams* have separate sessions for men and women, but the owners of *hammams* in tourist areas understand that visitors have different attitudes and will run mixed sessions. When you enter a *hammam* you are given a *peştama* (gown) and wooden sandals to wear. You can go naked under the robe or wear a swimming costume, bikini or shorts.

Then you go into the *hararet*, or steam room, where you are hit by a wall of hot air. Go to one of the basins and wash yourself all over. When you wash the suds off, do not get any back in the basin because this needs to be kept clean for other customers. You then lie on the *göbek taşi*, or naval stone, the marble slab at the centre of the room. Relax for 15 minutes or so to let the heat open up the pores.

Your masseur or *tellak* will then rub you with a rough cloth covered in soap to slough off any grime and dead skin cells. Then you are pummelled and rubbed until you feel as though your arms and legs might fall off. After another shower, you leave the hot room, wrap yourself in a thick robe and relax with a cup of tea. Do not rush this part because you need to cool down and let your body adjust to the treatment.

⬇ *A traditional Turkish bath is the perfect way to wind down*

Perge

The most complete ancient city so far discovered in the Turkish Mediterranean, the centre of Perge has been well excavated to reveal city streets, the remains of temples, shops and houses, and even a sophisticated communal air-conditioning system. The outskirts of the ancient site retain their allusive mystery, being shrouded in grasses and farmland.

Perge, founded around 1000 BC, was populated by the Pamphylians, who settled in the region and thrived on trade. It expanded under the Romans but declined under the Byzantines and Seljuks, and was eventually abandoned before the end of the first millennium AD.

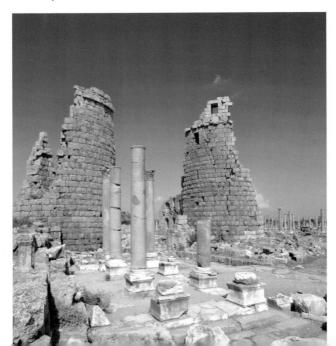

Archaeologists believe that much of the site remained intact until as recently as the beginning of the Turkish republic in the 1920s, when a building boom brought local people to trawl the site for stone they could use for their houses. ⓐ 29 km (18 miles) east of Antalya ⓛ Open 08.30–19.00 (May–Oct); 08.30–17.00 (Nov–Apr) ⓘ Admission charge

HIGHLIGHTS

Theatre ★★

Although not quite as impressive as Aspendos (see page 60), Perge's 2nd-century theatre is renowned for the fine friezes that adorned the stage wall – panels and theatre statues are on display in the Archaeological Museum in Antalya (see page 24). The theatre is usually closed due to archaeological excavations.

Stadium ★★★

This huge sporting arena, which is 234 m (256 yd) by 34 m (37 yd), with seating for 12,000 spectators, is the best example of its kind in the Mediterranean. The arcades under the terraces are believed to have housed shops and storage units.

Tomb of Plancia Magna ★

City records tell us that Plancia Magna was a great benefactress to the city, giving money for many public statues. Her tomb sits just outside the city gates beyond the ticket office. You can find a statue of her in the Museum of Archaeology at Antalya.

City gates ★★

There are two gates to the city. The Roman Gate is a simple entrance way, but the earlier Hellenistic Gate is the most prominent building at Perge. In a city of marble the gate is built of red stone and is made up of two round towers (now half ruined) fronting a horseshoe-shaped atrium. In the Roman period this gate was decorated with

◀ *The red stone Hellenistic Gate with remains of round towers* statues of the gods, but these are all now on display in the Antalya Archaeological Museum.

Roman baths ★

The impressive Roman baths complex is a good example of its kind. You can explore the *frigidarium* (cold room), *tepidarium* (warm room) and *caldarium* (hot room). Romans would move from one to the other to get the most beneficial treatment.

Roman agora ★

Across from the baths is the late-Roman *agora*, dating from the 4th century AD and constructed on a perfect square area measuring 75 sq m (82 sq yd).

Colonnaded street ★★

The main thoroughfare of the city, this wide marble lane was lined with Ionic columns and was cooled and freshened by a sophisticated water feature. A monumental fountain at the head of the street some thousand metres to the north fed a metre-high marble channel, running along the centre of the street all the way down to the square behind the Hellenistic Gate, with cold water that cooled the surrounding air. Halfway along, there is a marble bridge to allow traffic to cross from one side of the street to the other. Shops flanked both sides of the street. Each has a mosaic floor, and some floors are still in good condition. Today, local ladies spread their handmade lace and other souvenirs all along the colonnaded street – echoing the past.

Exploring the unexcavated areas ★

Once you leave the well-excavated colonnaded way you find yourself among wild tussock grasses. There are still buildings to explore, including an acropolis area, a necropolis and vestiges of the Roman walls that once surrounded the city.

◗ *Small, stone carved souvenirs on sale at Perge*

Aspendos

The theatre at the city of Aspendos is the most impressive single ancient monument along the Mediterranean coast.

Yet the city of Aspendos played a relatively minor role in ancient history. During Roman times it made its living from panning salt, but the site has had a long life because it was not finally abandoned until the 18th century. Of course, many of the monumental buildings were left to fall into disrepair long before this, and the same was true of the theatre – which was built during the reign of Roman Emperor Marcus Aurelius (AD 161–180). When Turkish President Kemal Atatürk visited Aspendos in the 1920s, he ordered that the theatre should be renovated and preserved for the nation.

⊚ 54 km (34 miles) south-west of Antalya **⊕** Open 08.30–19.00 (Apr–Oct); 08.30–17.00 (Nov–Mar) **ⓘ** Admission charge

Around the theatre you may be followed by touts selling 'Roman' coins. These are not genuine but copies of real coins, and make an unusual souvenir – provided you don't pay the 'very special' initial price asked by the touts.

HIGHLIGHTS
Theatre ★★★
This is one place where you could have stepped back in time. The theatre is just as it would have looked for Roman audiences and the bustle of your fellow visitors here gives an atmosphere of an audience arriving to take their seats for a performance. Built into a hillside in the classic Roman style (semi-circular with a huge stage wall), the theatre seating area, or *cavea*, has 40 rows of seats and can accommodate an audience of over 15,000 people. Topping the *cavea* there is an ornate vaulted gallery and upper walkway, or *ambulacrum*, from where you can look down on the whole structure.

The stage wall was used in Roman times to support stage scenery such as huge painted theatre backdrops. It once had monumental statuary in each of the niches but today these are empty and some of the statues are on display in the Archaeological Museum in Antalya (see page 24).

Legend of Aspendos Theatre A local legend states that the ruler of the city decreed that his daughter would be married to the man who could build the most beautiful and useful building for the city. Two men took up the challenge; one constructed the theatre, the other the aqueduct. The citizens could not decide who should take the prize and the king offered to share his daughter by cutting her in two. The builder of the theatre pulled out of the agreement, whereupon he was offered her hand.

Aspendos Opera and Ballet Festival The highlight of the arts calendar in the Mediterranean region, this festival is held in the theatre each June and features Turkish and foreign companies performing classic and experimental opera and ballet. It is a majestic sight when the theatre stage is dressed and the orchestra breaks the silence of the balmy evening – truly an unforgettable experience. Tickets are on sale at the theatre or in Antalya (see page 22). Ask at the tourist office because there is no permanent ticket office.

The view ★★★

For the best overall view of the interior, walk up the hill behind the theatre and you can look down into the whole structure. There are several dirt paths but they are steep in places so take care.

The city ★

Aspendos city has not been excavated and the remains of its once-great buildings lie floundering in the surrounding farmland. The most obvious are the huge *nymphaeum* (ornate facade of a public fountain) and early Christian basilica. Look out also for long sections of the aqueduct that brought fresh water to the city from the hills in the distance (a total of 15 km, or 9 miles, was originally built).

Rafting on the Köprülü Canyon

This is just about as energetic as you can get along the Turkish coast. Köprülü rafting is world famous, but the rapids are not really difficult – if you are a rafting virgin, this the perfect place to start. There is enough white water to get your adrenalin rushing, but lots of quiet spells in between for you to get your breath back and take in the wonderful views.

RAFTS

The large rafts can take around 15 people so they're perfect for a group. You get a guide who shows you the basics, and you are kitted out with safety gear. There is a bit of singing to get you in the party mood, before it's 'paddles at the ready'.

Just after you set off you come to the first set of rapids, but watch out. This is where the photographers stand to get your souvenir photograph – usually a great view of the shocked look on your face – so smile through the terror.

Medraft This is the longest-established rafting company.

ⓐ Yepibache Mah, Portakal Cecedi Bul, Huseyin Kuzu Apt 14/3, Antalya
ⓣ 0242 312 5770 ⓦ www.medraft.com ⓘ Children under six are not allowed to ride for safety reasons

KAYAKS

If the communal raft is not for you, you can hire one- and two-man kayaks and take the river at your own pace. Guided groups are great for beginners and novices because you have an experienced kayaker with you all the way.

KÖPRÜLÜ CANYON AREA

Upriver of the rafting base, the river snakes down from the foothills of the Taurus Mountains through a canyon, now protected as Köprülü Kanyon Milli Park (Köprülü Canyon National Park). You can explore this area on several footpaths.

All this excitement can really build up an appetite, so you'll be glad when it's lunchtime. At the canyon, there is a good choice of restaurants where you can enjoy a simple feast of barbecued meats and fresh trout with salads, followed by fruit, to replenish the energy levels.

◀ *Rafting on the Köprülü Canyon is for beginners and experts alike*

Termessos & the Karain Cave
a road trip

Still some way off the beaten tourist track, these two attractions, featuring some of Turkey's finest landscapes and a huge slice of ancient history, make a worthy day trip from the west of the region (Kemer, Antalya and Belek/Lara Beach).

There are few restaurants on your route so this trip provides the perfect chance to enjoy a picnic in the hills. There is lots of fresh fruit and vegetables plus delicious roast chicken and fresh bread in the local markets, or you can head to the the huge hypermarket in the Migros Shopping Centre in Antalya.

You need to head inland towards Burdur before taking a left towards Korkuteli after about 10 km (16 miles). The entrance to the Termessos site is on the left after about 15 km (9 miles). It is also signposted Güllük Dağ Milli Park (Güllük Mountain National Park). From the ticket office the approach road leads another 9 km (6 miles) through some wonderful Mediterranean scenery to the small car park at the base of the site. ❷ 34 km (21 miles) north-west of Antalya ● Open 08.30–19.00 (Apr–Oct); 08.30–17.00 (Nov–Mar) ❶ Admission charge; there are a few picnic tables close to the Termessos ticket office, which also has a small museum with a few finds and botanical information about the park. It can be worth having lunch before moving on.

TERMESSOS

The most dramatically sited ancient city along the Turkish coast, the ruins of ancient Termessos sit 1,000 m (3,281 ft) high in Güllük Dağ (Güllük Mountain Range), among granite crags and dense pine forest with magnificent views down to the coast in the south. Even in ancient times, Termessos was hard to reach, and so well sited for defensive purposes that even Alexander the Great could not conquer it. Termessos was built and populated by the Pisidians, who came from

🔺 *The impressive Roman amphitheatre at Termessos*

the central Anatolian plains. The remote location and impressive defences were two of the reasons why Alexander could not take the city during his campaign in 333 BC; another was the population, who spent the next couple of hundred years attacking the cities of the Lycian coast. Later they made a living extracting customs money from traders who had to take this route through the mountaina from the coast to central Turkey. They also signed an accord with the Romans that allowed them to keep their independence within the empire. The city was abandoned after an earthquake in the 3rd century AD and never resettled. Termessos has never been excavated, and its remains are only kept clear of vegetation by the constant stream of visitors, but do take care because there are no fences or other safety precautions at the site.

HIGHLIGHTS
Lower town ★
From the car park, you can examine the monumental Hadrian's Gate before beginning to climb uphill along the steep King's Road – this really sorts out the fit from the unfit. This was the main access way into the city and leads through two separate fortified walls.

Acropolis Plateau ★★
Once through the walls you reach the first plateau (after about twenty minutes' walking), which is effectively the centre of the city. Set among huge granite boulders, the buildings do not have the fine details of Perge (see page 56), but display a more rugged handsome strength. The gymnasium and baths complex are well preserved; there is a large mausoleum, a small stadium and the remains of several temples.

Theatre ★★★
Termessos theatre has the most impressive setting. Nestled in a rocky bowl, the cavea, or seating area, is not well preserved, but there is a breathtaking natural backdrop of the Mediterranean coastline, a thousand metres below.

Tomb of Alcatus ★★★

Alcatus was a leader of the Pisidians who defied the Greeks and committed suicide instead of being taken prisoner. This tomb has not been proved to be his, but the magnificent carved reliefs depicting a warrior on horseback date from around the time of his death in the early 3rd century BC and would be a fitting tribute to such an important man.

Necropolis ★★

This is a remarkable collection of tombs and sarcophagi dating from late in the city's history (1st–3rd century AD). A lookout tower is set at the highest point in the city. From here you can get excellent panoramic long-distance views of the coast from near Kemer to Antalya and beyond to the east.

KARAIN CAVE

The earliest Turks lived in this complex of caves set 65 m (213 ft) above sea level, in cliffs flanking a fertile valley to the north of Antalya. This is one of the richest Palaeolithic sites in the world, with 11 m (36 ft) of chronological remains allowing archaeologists to piece together the history of the region from *c.* 300,000 BC, when hippos, rhinos and elephants roamed free, to the present day.

The first humans came here 50,000 years ago and found it easy to hunt game and find fruit. Finds including tools and flints have helped to add a great deal to scientists' knowledge of our ancient relatives. The small museum has bones from ancient animals, including rhinos, hippos and smaller game that was obviously hunted by our early ancestors. The caves are a steep 20-minute hike up into the valley. There is a turning to Karain just outside the entrance to the Güllük Mountain National Park. From here it is 12 km (7 miles) to the Karain Cave. After the initial turning the road splits but comes back together again about 4 km (2.5 miles) further on. ⓐ 42 km (26 miles) north-west of Antalya ⓛ Open 08.30–18.00 ⓘ Admission charge

Myra (modern Demre/Kale)

The site at ancient Myra allows you go get up close to some of the best Lycian carved stone tombs in Turkey. The modern town of Kale (also known locally as Demre) close to the site has been a pilgrimage centre for many centuries because it is the birthplace of St Nicholas – Santa Claus or, as he is known in Turkey, Baba Noel.

HIGHLIGHTS

Dating back to the 5th century BC, Myra was one of the most important cities of the ancient Lycian people, supplying a form of incense to the expanding Greek and Roman world. The city was finally abandoned after earthquake damage and much of it remains to be excavated. Today there are three main areas to explore. 🚌 120 km (75 miles) south-west of Antalya, 2 km (1.2 miles) north of Kale/Demre centre 🕐 Open 08.30–19.30 (Apr–Oct); 08.30–17.00 (Nov–Mar) ❶ Admission charge

Sea Necropolis ★★★

This main collection of tombs is carved at eye level into the sheer cliff face. The tombs were carved to imitate the house of the subject during life, with an ornate door marking the entrance. You can get up close to the carvings to study the detail but you cannot go inside.

Theatre ★★

Next to the tombs is a well-preserved theatre, one of the smallest at a major site. The entrance galleries and stairs used by Roman audiences are still pretty much intact, so you can climb them and imagine you are going to take your seat for an ancient play. There are good views towards the sea from the vaulted upper walkway. The decorative friezes of theatrical muse masks that once framed the stage now lie scattered across the site.

▶ *The carved tombs of the Sea Necropolis at Myra*

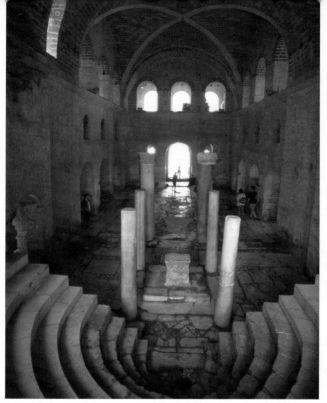

⬥ *The beautifully decorated Church of St Nicholas*

River Necropolis ✦ ✦

A less-visited group of tombs can be found to the right of the theatre,
a ten-minute walk from the main road through farmland. Known as the
River Necropolis because it faces the river (usually dried up in summer),
the most important tomb here is known as the 'Painted Tomb'. When
it was first discovered by explorers in the 1840s the tomb was covered
in bright pigment, but this has since disappeared. Even so, the reliefs
depicting a Lycian family group are still impressive.

Baba Noel Kilesi (The Church of St Nicholas) ★★★

Baba Noel Kilesi (The Church of St. Nicholas) is a church which is associated with St Nicholas. It was built in the 8th century to house the body of the saint, although this was later lost during a pirate raid in the 11th century.

It is an excellent and attractive example of the Byzantine or Romanesque style of architecture. Decorated with beautiful inlaid patterned floors featuring rare and expensive stones and marbles, the church is also worth visiting for its beautiful wall frescoes, the best of which can be seen close to the entrance.

The tomb said to be that of St Nicholas can be found in the southern aisle, although this is actually of a later date. However, there is another tomb of the correct date that is now on display in the Archaeological Museum in Antalya (see page 24). ⓐ 120 km (75 miles) south-west of Antalya; in the centre of the town ⓒ Open 08.30–19.00 (Apr–Oct); 08.30–17.00 (Nov–Mar) ❶ Admission charge

HOW PIOUS ST NICHOLAS BECAME JOLLY SANTA CLAUS

Christianity expanded quickly through the region after the 3rd century AD, and in the 4th century Myra became a bishopric. The first man to get the job was a local man, Nicholas, and he was said to have performed a number of miracles during his lifetime, including bringing several children back from the dead. He was made into a saint after his death.

The miracles St Nicholas performed made him the only sensible candidate for Patron Saint of Children and the 6 December was chosen as his saint's day. Over the centuries, in northern Europe and later in the United States, this religious St Nicholas gradually evolved into the jovial figure we know today, who wears his beard and robes because of the snowy December weather of the north.

Kekova boat trip

The coastal shallows of Kekova Sound in south-east Lycia make one of the most beautiful and popular trips along this part of the coast. Kekova Island shelters crystal-clear waters and numerous rocky islets. The vista is topped off by the jagged, arid Lycian peaks just inland.

Until recently, this idyllic corner of the Turkish coast was the exclusive preserve of 'yachties' who could lay anchor in one of the many remote coves seemingly miles away from the rest of the world. Today, the pleasures of the area can be enjoyed by everyone for a lot less than the cost of a yacht charter – and with lunch included in the package.
● Boat trips daily (weather permitting in winter) ❶ Admission charge (plus a charge for entering the castle)

The further you travel in a boat, the less time you'll have at Kekova, so you may not experience all the activities discussed below. The itinerary here assumes that you have sailed from the closest port, Üçağız, about 150 km (93 miles) west of Antalya. There are also cruises lasting several days from Antalya, which include Kekova on their itinerary.

HIGHLIGHTS
Kekova Island ★★
Kekova Island lies only a few hundred metres off shore and only became an island when the level of the Mediterranean rose in the early part of the first millennium. As the water flooded in, it swallowed the ancient city that thrived here. The boat sails in to view what remains of Batıkent (the 'sunken city') but archaeologists haven't yet identified which city it actually was.

The island is protected as an ancient site so no one is allowed to set foot on it, but your boat will get in close to shore and you can get good views of the remains of numerous stone buildings clinging to the hillside, and the ancient harbour just below the waterline. Under the water are the remains of yet more buildings, and the seabed is dotted with ancient pottery amphora lying where they fell many hundreds of years ago.

The necropolis of Teimiussa ★

On the inland shoreline are the remains of ancient Teimiussa, half-submerged in water and half-choked by the fertile mud that now helps make this part of Turkey the capital of fruit and vegetable production. Look out particularly for several excellent Lycian tombs rising out of the water, supported on their stone pillars.

Kaleköy ★★★

Kaleköy (the ancient site of Simena) is one of the prettiest and most authentic, untouched villages along the Turkish coast, and the view as you approach from the water makes a perfect picture, with a rash of traditional whitewashed houses climbing up the hillside, crowned by a sturdy fortress (see below).

Once your boat has moored at one of the numerous rustic wooden jetties, you are free to explore the narrow winding alleyways. The settlement is a fascinating mixture of living community and tourist town. Most of the houses are family homes and chickens roam free throughout the village, scattering noisily as you approach. The older women sit in their doorways crocheting or making the lace that is on sale everywhere; children offer fruit or small trinkets, while carpet shops simply hang their wares off balconies or over walls.

The Fortress of the Knights of St John ★★

Tours usually include a visit to this fortress, built by the Knights of St John and offering wonderful high-level views over the sound and down over the town. It's one of their smaller outposts, but still a beautiful example of crusader architecture. 🕐 24 hours ❶ Admission charge when guardian is on duty

Swimming ★

After your explorations, you will be allowed time for swimming and snorkelling. Watch out for the spiny sea urchins that breed in the shallows here. If you step on them, the spines break off in your foot and can become infected.

Olymbos & Chimaera

Most easily reached from the western Mediterranean resorts but worth the trip from the others, the narrow coastal strip south of Kemer is hemmed in against the sea by high, pine-clad cliffs, and even in the late 1990s it was still remote from the rest of Turkey. It was regarded as a hippy or backpacker destination with simple accommodation in tree houses and cabins for the few who ventured here – almost like a Turkish version of the film *The Beach*. Today, the bay makes a popular boat trip from around the coast, and the newly upgraded road has improved access for cars.

OLYMBOS (OLYMPOS)

Olymbos beach ★★★

One of the finest on the stretch of coast that includes the good beaches of Kemer and Beldibi, Olymbos is particularly beautiful because it is still backed by lush vegetation, not concrete hotels. There are a few cafés under the pines and a village centre at Çıralı, but no high-rise buildings to spoil the natural view. It is especially dramatic against the mountainous backdrop only a few hundred metres inland.

Olymbos site ★★

Ancient Olymbos occupied a spectacular site by a natural spring close to the beach. Named after nearby Mount Olymbos – now Tahtalı Dağ – it was an important Lycian town dating from around 200 BC. The chief god of the town was Hephaistos (known to the Romans as Vulcan), patron of fire and of blacksmiths. This was obviously a direct result of the natural flames of Chimaera close by (see opposite). The site continued to be occupied after the fall of Rome and was an important port for the Byzantines and the Genoese between the 7th and 14th centuries.

Today the unexcavated site is rather a jumble in the verdant vegetation. The Byzantine and Genoese walls and fortifications at the seaward end of the site are among the most obvious structures. The city was a target for pirates throughout the first millennium so the fortifications were very necessary.

Just below the harbour fortifications are the Harbour Tombs, two Lycian funerary monuments, one of which has had its inscription translated into English. Explore further inland on the well-worn paths to find scant remains of warehouses, villas and a theatre.

Until recently, the fresh water that surrounds and sometimes submerges the site was a haven for wildlife such as frogs, birds and insects, but since it has become more popular and the water quality has been spoiled by sun lotions and litter left by visitors who should know better, they have all but disappeared. ⓐ 75 km (47 miles) south-west of Antalya ⓒ Open 08.30–19.00 (Apr–Oct); 08.30–17.00 (Nov–Mar) ❶ Admission charge

CHIMAERA

The natural flames rising out of the rocks on Tahtalı Dağ peak have been seen since ancient times. Then, sailors thought that they were the breath of the chimaera – the monster with a lion's front, a goat's rear and a dragon's tail. The Turks call the flames *yanartaş*, or 'burning rock'. Greek myth tells us that the chimaera was killed when Bellerophon dropped molten lead into its mouth, but the flames still burn – although they have been a little diminished over the centuries and are certainly not visible from offshore any more.

It is a 20-minute walk into the hills from the car park at the ticket office, but if you have arrived on a boat trip you should allow an hour to walk from Çıralı village (a three-hour round trip with time to view the flames). Most of the flames do not rise much above calf height and many of them are very transparent, so take care not to get burned as you clamber over the rocks. ⓐ 75 km (47 miles) south-west of Antalya ⓒ 24 hours – a ticket office is staffed daily 08.30–19.00 (Apr–Oct); 08.30–17.00 (Nov–Mar) ❶ There is an admission charge when the ticket office is open

Pamukkale

Pamukkale (Pamuk-alay) means 'cotton castle' in Turkish, and it is a most appropriate name. This huge natural travertine fountain is one of the country's most famous attractions and one of its most beautiful and spectacular landscapes. Terraces of shallow limestone pools the shape of oyster shells cling to the hillside like a giant, stepped pool against the blue sky. From a distance it looks like piles of raw cotton; close up, the limestone is brilliant white and its edges glitter like diamonds – so don't forget your sunglasses! It's an overnight trip inland from the Mediterranean coast, but well worth a visit.

HIGHLIGHTS
The Travertine Cascades ★★★
Several storeys of pure white shallow bowls are filled with azure blue waters shimmering in the sunshine. ❷ 265 km (165 miles) north-west of Antalya ● 24 hours (ticket office manned during daylight hours) ❶ Admission fee charged when ticket office manned

Hierapolis ★★
The Romans loved natural springs. They thought they could cure various ailments. Hierapolis, the city they built here on top of the plateau next to Pamukkale, was really a giant spa town. Walk down the Cardo, the colonnaded main street to the Gate of Dominitian, or explore the

⬤ *Lean against Roman columns at Pamukkale's thermal baths*

SAVING PAMUKKALE

In the early days, there was no protection for Pamukkale's delicate environment. People broke the sides of the pools as they climbed over them and sun oils from swimmers left a residue in the water that discoloured the white limestone. To add to this, several hotels that were built above the cascade began to use water from the spring for their own swimming pools, so it wasn't reaching the limestone pools to repair the damage. By the early 1990s 'cotton castle' was in real danger.

In the mid 1990s, the Turkish authorities instigated an action plan to save the Cascades. The hotels on the plateau have been bulldozed and the waters are being trained over the most damaged sections to make them white once again, a bit like the now-popular teeth whitening process. People have been banned from bathing in or walking on the pools. There is a footpath you can follow as long as you take your shoes off, but it is a bit painful for soft feet! All these changes have made a huge difference, and the total area of white limestone has begun to expand again.

Necropolis (cemetery), with its collection of more than 1,200 tombs and giant sarcophagi. The **museum** on site displays a range of items found during the excavation. ❶ Extra ticket charge

Pamukkale Thermal Baths ★★★
These baths have been open since Roman times and the modern buildings have been built directly on top of the ancient ones. While you are bathing, you can sit on fallen Roman columns that lie just under the surface of the water. The warm springs are said to be good for arthritis, stress and a long list of other ailments – although most people just come for the fun of swimming there. Even if you do not want to get wet (extra charge), come and have a look at the pools. ❶ Open 09.00–20.00

Ephesus

The largest and most complete ancient city in the eastern Mediterranean, Ephesus is a must-see site. The exceptionally well-preserved buildings, with little touches that bring the citizens to life, allow us to step back in time to the late Roman era, when this was the capital of Asia Minor. It's a long trip from the Mediterrean region, over 500 km (310 miles) west of Antalya, and at least one overnight stay is necessary. Tours often include visits to Pamukkale and other sites.

HISTORY

Founded in the 11th century BC, Ephesus became an important and rich city because it was the centre of worship for the goddess of fertility, Artemis. The temple here was one of the Seven Wonders of the Ancient World and attracted pilgrims from around ancient Greece.

In Roman times, the city was capital of Asia Minor with a population of over 250,000. It was a trading and banking city of immense wealth and was one of the most advanced cities in the Empire, with both flushing communal latrines and street lighting.

It was an important Christian city with a close association with St Paul of Tarsus and was populated until the 11th century AD. The last few hundred years brought serious problems when its port on the River Cayster began to silt up. Eventually it was cut off from the sea completely, making trade impossible. The city was then abandoned.

HIGHLIGHTS

Upper City ★

A plateau at the top of the hill is the least exciting part of the city. Around the wide space that was once the Upper Agora, you will be able to explore the administrative headquarters, a small *odeon* (theatre) and the remains of a thermal spa. The best part of the upper city is the view down over the rest of Ephesus. From the small square in front of the Monument of Memmius, which was erected in homage to the citizens of the city, you get a most breathtaking view down Curetes Street, one of the most photographed vistas in Turkey. Beyond, look out over the flat area where there is a modern airfield. This used to be port for the ancient city. Take some time to search for the coast in the distance. This is how far the sea has receded since Roman times and shows why the city was doomed; with no way to transport goods overland, it couldn't function.

Curetes Street ★★★
The major arterial route linking the upper city with the port, Curetes Street had shops selling goods from around the empire, along with a number of important temples. These include the Temple of Hadrian (built *c.* AD 117–138), with its distinctive double archway of fine Corinthian columns and an elaborate frieze dedicated to the goddess Tyche.

Slope House ★★★
On each side of Curetes Street, the residential quarters of Ephesus lie on the terraced hillside, reached by narrow alleyways. These were the houses of the rich, and one three-storey residence, Yamac Evleri or 'Slope House', has undergone a thorough excavation to offer a glimpse of the Roman lifestyle and interior design. The spacious rooms are decorated with incredible original mosaic floors and wall frescoes that were the height of fashion. ❶ Extra admission charge, but it is worth it.

Gate of Mazeus and Mithridates ★★
Linking the library and the neighbouring *agora*, the Gate of Mazeus and Mithridates was commissioned by two slaves freed by the Emperor Augustus who went on to become leading citizens of the city. It is built in the style of a triumphal arch.

Celcus Library ★★★
At the bottom of Curetes Street, the library is one of the focal points of the city. Erected in AD 117 as a memorial to Tiberius Julius Celsus by his son, it has a grandiose two-storey facade decorated with fluted

● *The grand Celcus Library*

columns and statues depicting The Four Virtues: Goodness (*Arete*), Thought (*Ennoia*), Knowledge (*Episteme*) and Wisdom (*Sophia*). The library once held 12,000 scrolls and was considered a great centre of learning.

Baths of Scolastica ★

The baths were one of the social centres of the city, a place where men got together to do business deals, debate politics or simply gossip. These were built in the 1st century AD in the heart of the city almost opposite the Celcus Library, and you can still see the hot room and cold room.

Theatre ★★★

One of the prettiest and most complete Roman theatres, Ephesus theatre is still used during the important Ephesus Festival of Culture and Art each May. During Roman times, 24,000 people would cram the stands to enjoy drama and comedy, but it was also the scene of many of St Paul's Evangelical speeches. He was cornered here by angry Ephesians when he criticized their beloved Artemis, but managed to escape.

Arcadian Way ★

One of the first Roman streets to get municipal lighting (in the 5th century AD), Arcadian Way led from the theatre to the port. The widest avenue in the city, much of it is now off limits, but it is possible to stand at the top (in front of the theatre) and look towards what would have been the warehouse district and the waterfront during Roman times.

Marble Way ★

Linking Curetes Street with Arcadian Way, the short Marble Way has a couple of interesting things to see. Notice how the marble of the road surface has been worn away by the passing of hundreds of thousands of cart wheels. No doubt these carts were heavily laden with goods for market. There is also an advertisement for a brothel etched in a stone of the road, pointing the way to the entrance close by.

Temple of Artemis ★

A kilometre away from the city is the Temple of Artemis or Artemision, the most important temple to Artemis in the ancient world. A mammoth building, it houses a life-size gold statue to the goddess. It was so impressive that it was known as one of the Seven Wonders of the Ancient World, but today it is a shadow of its former self. The Goths destroyed the site in AD 262 and much of the stone was later recycled – only the main temple platform and a couple of lonely columns remain. Although the statue has never been found, there are several stone and marble statues of her in the Ephesus Museum at Selçuk (see below).

Ephesus Museum ★★★

If you visit the site of Ephesus, you must also visit the Ephesus Museum in the nearby town of Selçuk (Selchuk). This is where the best of the artefacts found at the site are on display.

The museum is not too big and overwhelming and includes the re-creation of a Roman room excavated at the site, complete with furniture and a small domestic shrine. The range of everyday objects on display is impressive, from hair pins to leather sandals. More precious objects include gold filigree jewellery and fine Samian tableware.

Several rooms display monumental statuary and friezes that decorated temples and public buildings, as well as the Hall of the Emperors, where statues and busts of many Roman leaders have been brought together. ❸ 129 km (80 miles) north of Marmaris. Agora Çarşısı, Selçuk ⏰ Open 08.30–noon and 13.30–17.30 ❶ Admission charge

○ *Rock homes cut into the volcanic tufa at Cappadocia*

Cappadocia

It is a day's journey from the Mediterranean coast inland to Cappadocia and you should spend at least a night in the area (accommodation is often included in the price). This is one of Turkey's most fascinating regions for its spectacular natural landscapes, its religious treasures and its modern-day rural lifestyles.

A total contrast to the verdant pine forests and farmland of the coast, at first Cappadocia seems like a vast expanse of white stone devoid of any life. In fact, it is a very fertile region famed for its wine and, in years gone past, for its horses. Methods of farming have not changed much for generations because the narrow valleys that shelter the fields do not allow for mass production. Donkeys and mules are used as a matter of course here, rather than trucks or tractors. Families live comfortably in their small, rock-cut homes. Further caves provide storage rooms and shelter for livestock.

During the Byzantine era (4th–11th centuries AD), the region had a thriving Christian community with several important monasteries. The concentration of early churches and their wall paintings (frescoes) represents one of the most important collections of religious art and architecture in the world.

THE CHRISTIAN ERA

St Paul introduced Christianity to Cappadocia as early as the first century AD when he passed through here on his evangelical journeys. The community grew quietly away from the gaze of Pagan Rome, then flourished when Christianity was declared the legal religion of the empire. As time passed, this region was on the north-east outskirts of safe Christian territory and was prone to Arab raids from the east – that is the reason why so many churches were hidden from view in narrow and remote valleys.

HOW THE LANDSCAPE WAS CREATED

The whole Cappadocia region used to be volcanic and is covered with a layer of soft grey-white volcanic rock called tufa. It is easily worn away by rain and wind, and over the centuries these forces have fashioned the beautiful and surreal shapes, revealing layers of differing colours and the rounded curves and towers seen all across the region.

FAIRY CHIMNEYS

Most famous of the Cappadocian features are the 'fairy chimneys'. These are created when a layer of hard rock sits on top of a layer of tufa. Over time rain gets into the cracks of the harder rock and washes away the tufa below, except that situated directly underneath the hard rock. Eventually, as more tufa gets washed away, all that is left is a tall column with a rock hat on top.

HISTORY

Cappadocia has been swept up in the east-to-west movement of the great empires over the last 4,000 years. It was the centre of the Hittite Empire from *c.* 1800 to 1200 BC before the Persians became overlords. Then the Romans arrived and built a regional capital, Caesarea, at what is now the town of Kayseri.

Following the division of the Roman Empire in the 4th century, Cappadocia became part of the Christian Byzantine Empire with its capital at Constantinople (now Istanbul). The Seljuk Muslims arrived from the east during the 12th century, followed by the Ottomans in the 15th century, but the region became a backwater under Islam.

In 1907, a French priest rediscovered the early churches during an expedition through the Turkish hinterland, but it was not until the late 1980s that Cappadocia became part of the established tourist trail.

● *Cappadocian 'fairy chimneys' – natural formations created through erosion*

THINGS TO SEE & DO

Avanos ★

Set on the Red River, Avanos is famed for the distinctive red pottery made from the clay of the surrounding hills that has been around since Hittite times. The old town with its Ottoman and Greek mansions is a splendid place for a stroll and some shopping ⓐ 12 km (7 miles) north of Göreme

Balloon ride ★★★

A hot-air balloon ride allows the best views of the marvellous shapes and contours of the unique landscape. You depart at dawn (weather permitting), and glide effortlessly along for around an hour or so before landing to enjoy a celebratory glass of bubbly with your breakfast.
Kapadokya Balloons A long-running company, with experienced, multilingual pilots and an excellent safety record. ⓐ Adnan Menderes Caddesi, Goreme ① 0384 271 2442 Ⓦ www.kapadokyaballoons.com

⬆ *Walk amongst rock-cut Byzantine churches at Göreme Open-Air Museum*

Derinkuyu ★★★

Cappadocia has a whole collection of underground settlements
carved from the tufa to allow the local populations to live in safety
from invading forces. These cities are thought to be much older than
the rock-cut churches – perhaps even dating back to Hittite times.

The best-excavated of the cities is Derinkuyu, meaning 'deep well' in
Turkish. Eight storeys have been studied so far – that is over 50 m (164 ft)
underground – but archaeologists estimate that this is only a quarter
of the whole city. Here, you can explore how the people lived their lives,
with stables for livestock, kitchens, dining rooms and churches.
Sophisticated ventilation brought fresh air in and let stale air and
smoke escape, while the wells after which the town is now named
provided a constant supply of water. ⓐ 40 km (25 miles) south of
Göreme ⓛ Open 08.00–19.00 (July–Sep); 08.00–17.00 (Oct–Apr);
08.00–17.00 (May–Jun) ⓘ Admission charge

Göreme Village ★

Göreme is now a tourist town with a mass of pensions, cafés, shops and tour operators, but it is set among the most beautiful and typical tufa landscapes. Just a short walk or drive out of the centre you can find people still living in their rock houses growing vines and keeping livestock in the sheltered valleys.

Göreme Open-Air Museum ★★★

This World Heritage Site now protects some of the finest treasures of Cappadocia, a cluster of over 30 rock-cut Byzantine churches and chapels that represents the development of religious art between the 4th and 11th centuries, and paints a picture of how the Christian community lived during its years of relative isolation. Whenever you visit, one or more of these churches will probably be closed for renovation because they are both precious and fragile. Each has something to offer, but listed below are some of the highlights. ⓐ 2 km (1 mile) north of Göreme ⓛ Open 08.30–17.30 (Apr–Oct); 08.30–17.00 (Nov–Mar) ⓘ Admission charge

Elmalı Kilise (Apple Church) The most famous of the churches, Apple Church is decorated with stunning and colourful frescoes depicting Christ Pantocrator (enthroned) surrounded by angels. These 11th-century images are some of the latest in the museum and show a sophistication of imagery and development of artistic style. Look also for the simple red-ochre decoration added during the iconoclastic period (the 8th and early 9th centuries), which was a time when decorating churches with images of the saints was frowned upon.

Yılanlı Kilise (Church of the Snakes) This church is renowned for its depiction of the early Byzantine saints. These include ruler Constantine and his mother St Helena holding the True Cross, St Onophrius who lived as a hermit in the Egyptian desert and the martyr St Theodore, a Roman soldier who refused to renounce Christ and worship the pagan Roman gods.

Karanlık Kilise (Dark Church) The lack of light in this church preserved the vivid colour of the frescoes, and with a well-managed renovation programme in the 1990s these are now the pride of the collection. They also give the greatest indication of how the other churches would have looked in their heyday. One of the most dramatic frescoes to look out for is the Betrayal of Judas and Christ Crucified.

ⓘ Admission charge

New Church This church holds some of the best Christian frescoes in the Byzantine world, including 10th-century images depicting scenes from the life of Christ. These hark back to the early, pre-Iconoclastic era, but there is a new realism in the figures – shown by shading and layering in the paintings – displaying a development in style over the period. The most evocative scenes are the Descent from the Cross and Passion and Resurrection.

Uçhisar ★★

The village is dominated by the Uçhisar rock, a massive 60 m (197 ft) dome of tufa that was once a living community. It is almost like a gigantic 3-D puzzle that you can actually climb into. Every inch of it has been carved to create living space and the views are spectacular. You can explore the cobbled streets of this farming community, complete with tethered donkeys and flocks of chickens and geese.

ⓐ 4 km (2.5 miles) south-west of Göreme � Open 08.00–20.30

ⓘ Admission charge

SHOPPING

Cappadocia is one of the best places in Turkey to buy a genuine antique or carpet. Although prices are not necessarily any cheaper than on the coast, there is a better choice and your souvenir will certainly be unique.

● *Cappadocia's churches have some of the world's best Christian frescoes*

Zelve Open-Air Museum ★★

Originally a large Christian monastery, the carved rock complex in the three valleys that make up Zelve were inhabited as late as the 1950s. Several levels of rooms can be seen – you can climb the metal stairs to explore some sections – but there are very few fine frescoes here. The simple painted crosses in the chapels indicate that the complex was decorated during the Iconoclastic era. ● 8 km (5 miles) north-east of Göreme ● Open 08.00–19.00 (Apr–Oct); 08.00–17.00 (Nov–Mar) ● Admission charge

EXCURSIONS

Lara Beach

Lara Beach has to be Mediterranean Turkey's next full-blown resort. Up until now it has really been classed as a suburb of Antalya (it is only a few kilometres to the west), and many of the city dwellers head here at weekends to enjoy the fantastic beach and water sports.

There are many informal beach bars backing the strand, so you can simply spend the day on the beach, but Lara has other attractions, including what was Turkey's first water park (❸ Dedeman Hotel, Lara Yolu ❶ 0212 275 7600 ⓦ www.depark.com.tr). This has a range of rides, pools and activities for adults and children of all ages. The Dedeman Hotel also has a bowling alley, which is pretty unusual for Turkey, and might make a change for a family evening out.

Selge

If you head further up into the hills beyond the Köprülü rafting base you pass into the Köprülü Canyon National Park (see page 62), an area of pine-clad granite peaks blanketed in wild scrub and herbs. Few tour buses find their way here, so although you are not far from the resorts, this is true natural Turkey. After 7 km (4 miles) you reach a small village called Altınköy. Here, people are still making a living from farming, and the women sit in their doorways crocheting or making lace.

Scattered around the village are the remains of ancient Selge, once a city with a population of over 20,000 people. The site has not been excavated, but well-worn paths lead to the major buildings, which include a partly buried agora and atmospheric theatre.

If you need a guide, inquire in the village – one of the local men will show you around for a small fee. ❸ 55 km (34 miles) from the 400 coast road, 7 km (4 miles) from rafting station ❶ 24 hours, informal ticket sales in village ❶ Admission charge when ticket seller is in the area

Food & drink

Turkish cuisine is considered to be one of the greatest in the world. Just like French or Chinese cuisine, it has had a huge influence on both what we eat and how we eat it. Though the days of the great Ottoman banquets are long gone, Turks still make meal times an event.

Freshness is the key to Turkish food – you need only look at the mountains of seasonal fruit and vegetables on sale in local markets or the seafood on ice at harbour-front restaurants for evidence of this. Dishes are generally cooked in olive oil, and a range of herbs and spices have traditionally been used to add flavour, but these are never overpoweringly strong.

WHEN TO EAT

Turks take a very relaxed approach to meal times. There will always be somewhere open no matter what time you get hungry, though you will find most atmosphere between noon and 14.30 for lunch and between 19.00 and 22.00 for dinner, when other people head out to eat. Only the most formal restaurants close between lunch and dinner, and eateries of all kinds tend to stay open until the last client leaves.

In Turkey, food is usually served warm rather than hot, which usually means chips arrive soggy not crisp. If you want yours piping hot, tell the waiter when you order.

WHERE TO EAT

Choosing these different styles of eateries depends on your appetite:
Kahve A Turkish coffee house that does not serve food and is usually a place for the men to get together for a game of backgammon or a gossip.
Lokanta A casual, often family-owned restaurant serving a small range of home-cooked dishes. There probably will not be a printed menu, but it is normal to go into the kitchen to see what is being cooked. Point at what you want if the staff do not speak English.

Restoran A more formal restaurant than a *lokanta*. A *restoran* will have a printed menu with prices.

Kebapçi Specializes in grilled meats. They vary from pretty, family-owned establishments with outdoor terraces to small, urban kiosks.

Meyhane A bar- or pub-style place serving meze with drinks. These have traditionally been for males only, but in tourist areas women will also be welcomed.

Pideçi These small snack bars serve Turkish pizza.

Bufes A basic snack bar.

Pastane Turkish patisseries serving cakes and pastries.

WHAT TO EAT

Meze dishes or starters

Turks prefer to eat *meze* style. That is where several small dishes are served at once and shared by everyone around the table. Try eating *meze* style for a truly authentic experience, or order these dishes to have as a starter.

Cold options include *yaprak dolması* (stuffed vine leaves), fresh olives, *imam bayildi* (slices of aubergine with tomatoes and onions in olive oil) and *cacık* (a refreshing dip of natural yoghurt and cucumber with a hint of mint). Warm *meze* dishes include *borek* (filo pastry squares filled with cheese and herbs) and *midye dolması* (stuffed mussels)

Because Turks eat *meze* style (see above), you may find that if you order starters and main courses they will both arrive together. To avoid this, order only one course at a time.

Main courses

The most popular form of main course is grilled or barbecued meat, usually lamb, but you will also find some beef. It is grilled as chops or steak but also cubed and skewered for *şiş kebabs*, thinly sliced for *döner kebabs* or minced for *köfte* (meat balls) or *İskender kebab* (minced meat wrapped around a skewer). Meat is always fresh and is generally served cooked through, not pink in the middle or rare.

Fresh fish is plentiful and delicious. You will find it elaborately displayed on ice at restaurant entrances. It is, however, always the most expensive item on the menu. It is sold by weight, so you choose a fish and it will be weighed and priced for you, then cooked to your specifications. If you find the price beyond your budget you get the chance to change your mind before it is too late.

You will normally find that your main meal comes with bread and salad and either rice or chips.

Snacks

Turkey has excellent pizza (*pide* or *lahmacun*), though it is lighter than the Italian variety and often served rolled up so you can eat it on the go. Equally delicious are *döner kebabs*, slivers of lamb wrapped with salad in pitta bread, and you can find these on almost every street corner. *Gözleme* are pancakes or crepes with sweet or savoury fillings, while *semit* (bread rings sprinkled with sesame seeds) are perfect for stopping those afternoon hunger pangs.

Sweets

Turkish sweets and puddings are world renowned and make no apology for the amount of calories they contain. The most famous, *baklava* – layers of filo pastry soaked in butter, sprinkled with nuts then baked in honey syrup – is a work of art. Milk puddings are also popular, and are often delicious rich rice puddings evoking those we enjoyed as children. *Lokum* or Turkish delight (a jelly sweet traditionally flavoured with rose water, but you will find many fruit flavours today) makes a great accompaniment to Turkish coffee.

If all this really sounds a little over the top, most *lokanta* and *restoran* offer fresh melon or other seasonal fruit as a lighter but equally delicious end to your meal. The sweet toothed will need to head to a specialist café for dessert. These are often very basic establishments with vinyl-topped tables and fluorescent lights, so they do not get points for romantic ambience, but they are full of authentic atmosphere.

International food

More and more 'international' food has become available in Turkey. This includes all-day English breakfasts if that's what you want, as well as other familiar items like pizzas and burgers. If you want to splash out, the large, upmarket hotels will have formal and expensive restaurants serving 'continental' menus with silver service.

Drinks

The usual array of fizzy soft drinks and international spirits are readily available, so you will certainly find something familiar during your trip. But why not try a particularly Turkish beverage? *Khave*, or Turkish coffee, is strong but never harsh and served in small cups. Take it *sade* (no sugar), *az şekerli* (a little sugar) or *çok şekerli* (sweet), but never try to empty the cup because there are grounds in the bottom. *Çay* (tea) is served weak without milk in tulip-shaped glasses. Apple tea is a refreshing alternative. Another delicious non-alcoholic drink is *ayran*, a refreshing natural-yoghurt drink. Bottled water is also readily available (don't drink water from the tap).

Turkey produces some excellent wine. Look for the trade names Doluca and Kavaklıdere for quality and reliability. It also brews a good, clean-tasting Pilsen-type beer under the brand name Efes, but for something more potent try *raki*, an anis-based spirit that is diluted with water. It is taken as both a before- or after-dinner drink, but at a strength of 40 per cent, should always be taken in moderation.

TIPPING

Most *restoran* will add 10–15 per cent to your bill, but you should still leave a little something for the waiter. *Lokantas* will normally not add service to the bill. It is customary to leave 10–15 per cent. Leave small change on the table at bars and coffee houses.

LIFESTYLE

Menu decoder

A FEW BASIC WORDS

alabalık Freshwater trout

aşure Sweet 'soup' of fruits, nuts, pulses and bulgar wheat

balık Fish

barbunya Red mullet

beyti Minced kebab in pitta bread

bonfile Steak

borek Savoury pastry usually with cheese filling but can be meat

bülbül yuvası (swallow's nest) Shredded wheat in sugar syrup

çay Tea

çöp kebap Finely chopped meat or offal

dolma Vine leaves stuffed with rice and herbs

döner kebab Thin slices of grilled lamb sliced from a cone of meat

ekmek Bread

fasulye Haricot beans in tomato sauce

fırında sütlaç Oven-baked rice pudding usually served cold

gözleme A wafer-thin crepe with sweet or savoury filling

güllaç Flaky pastry and milk flavoured with nuts and rose water

güveç Meat and/or vegetable stew, cooked in a clay pot.

hamsi Anchovies

haydarı Yoghurt dip flavoured with garlic

imam bayıldı Translated as 'the imam fainted' – a classic Ottoman dish
of baked aubergine with tomatoes and onions served cold

istakoz Lobster

İskander kebab Minced meat cooked around a skewer and served in
yoghurt or tomato sauce

kabak tatlısı Baked squash topped with clotted cream (*kaymak*)

kalamar Squid

karides Shrimp

karışık ızgara Mixed grill of lamb meat

karnıyarık Aubergines stuffed with minced lamb, currants and pine nuts
then baked

karpuz Watermelon

kayısı Apricot

khave Turkish coffee

kiraz Cherry

kuzu Lamb

lahmacun A wafer-thin pizza topped with tomato sauce and minced lamb

levrek Sea bass

maden su Mineral water

manti Noodle dough ravioli parcels filled with meat

menemen Stir-fried omelette with hot peppers and vegetables

mercimak çorbası Lentil soup

midye Mussel

pastırma Dry-cured beef served thinly sliced

pide Small, flat pizzas with a thin topping of minced lamb or cheese

piliç Roast chicken

pirzola Lamb chops

pilav Rice

piyaz Haricot beans in vinaigrette

portakal Orange

salata Salad

şarap Wine

sardalya Sardine

sığır Beef

şiş kebab Cubes of meat put on a skewer then grilled

su Water

süt Milk

tarama Pink fish-roe paste

tavuk Boiled chicken

tel kadayıf Shredded wheat base smothered in honey syrup and chopped nuts

turşu Pickled vegetables

tuz Salt

yayla çorbası Rice soup

yoğurt çorbası Yoghurt soup

Shopping

There is something for everyone in Mediterranean Turkey, with a whole range of excellent souvenirs in all price brackets. You will be bombarded with designer rip-offs offering those must-have names at a fraction of the price back home. Stock up on items by your favourite fashion house, but check merchandise carefully, as quality varies from good to terrible.

Leather is also one of the top-ten buys for tourists. You will find a fantastic range of bags, belts and jackets. Again, designer names predominate but you can find traditional styles or have something made just for you.

Turkey is famous for its handicrafts and these include inlaid wooden items like small tables or chess sets, copper pots, rustic ceramics and pottery, onyx or Meerschaum pipes carved from a hard white clay found only in Turkey.

Gold and silver jewellery is also good value as items such as chains and bracelets are priced by weight. You can have things made at small jewellery workshops within a few days. Gold is usually 14-carat quality. Always check for the hallmark on gold and silver items.

The prize souvenir has to be the handmade Turkish carpet. These have been woven for centuries – each region has traditional patterns and colours. The best are made of silk, but most are wool.

Kilims are different to carpets because they have a flat weave rather than a pile. These are just as colourful but generally cheaper and they make great rugs and throws.

BROWSING

Browsing and window-shopping are not things the Turks do. When a shopkeeper sees you looking at his wares, he assumes you have an interest in buying. Obviously, they would rather you buy from them than from the shop next door, so they will put a lot of effort into getting you to stop, look and try.

BARTERING

Bartering or bargaining is a fact of life in Turkey. It is not something that comes naturally to a shopper who is used to fixed prices, but that doesn't mean it is something to be nervous or worried about. If you are in the market to buy an expensive souvenir such as a leather jacket or a Turkish carpet, you will be paying well over the odds if you simply pay what the shopkeeper asks.

⬥ *Turkish markets are always busy*

There are several tips to make the bartering process more successful and enjoyable.

To start with, act cool about the specific item you want. Look at several items and then perhaps tell the shopkeeper you want to look in other shops to compare goods.

You will be offered a drink – Turkish tea or a soft drink – and it shows that you are more serious about buying if you accept.

Your first offer should be around 50 per cent of what the shop owner asks, then increase your offer little by little. You will probably end up paying around 70 per cent of the original asking price, but early or late in the season it could be more.

If you don't want to pay the price, simply tell the shop owner and walk away. He may call you back with a lower offer. Once you agree a price it is very bad manners to change your mind!

You will get a better price if you pay in cash rather than with a credit card, and better still if you pay in pounds sterling or euros rather than in Turkish Lira.

Kids

Turkey is an ideal destination for children. The simple pleasures of guaranteed sunshine, excellent beaches and warm water to play in will keep them happy for hours. Add to this the child-friendly environment, where children are welcomed in restaurants and cafés, and it makes for a very relaxed holiday. Exuberance is not frowned upon here. Turks love children and allow them the freedom to enjoy their childhood.

That said, you will find fewer attractions specifically aimed at children than in many European destinations. There are no children's museums, few 'theme' parks and no games arcades. But the jet skiing and water rides make up for that, as well as the chance to spot a wild dolphin or turtle during a boat trip.

TIPS FOR A CHILD-FRIENDLY TRIP

Turkish excursions can be heavy on history, and even the most enthusiastic adults can tire of this. Pace the sightseeing so you can alternate days of gazing at ancient buildings and tramping ancient streets with days by the pool or on the beach.

An afternoon siesta will help young children stay up late with the Turkish kids (who are often still playing in town squares until midnight). Early afternoon is also a good time to hide from the sun (see below).

THE MEDITERRANEAN

The Mediterranean has pretty varied activities for children. It has more child-friendly beaches than any other region in Turkey, with excellent strands at Lara Beach close to Antalya, beaches around Side and the gorgeous bays at Alanya. Here, they can have the full range of water sports to enjoy, including fast-paced banana rides or the opportunity for quieter sea kayaking in the coastal shallows.

Fresh water provides the most exhilarating experience at **Köprülü Canyon** (see page 62), where older children can ride the rapids in relative

● *Turkey's many ancient buildings provide fascinating insights into history*

safety. Antalya's refurbished waterfront area – **Antalya Beach Park** (see page 24) – has a collection of child-friendly activities, the most exciting of which is the swim with the dolphins programme at **Dolphinland**. There is a water park and a recreation area, plus lots of shady forest to play in. Other water parks can be found between Alanya (see page 12) and Side (see page 32).

Jeep safaris (see page 52) are great fun for older children. Routes take you off road and offer a real 'Indiana Jones' experience.

BEWARE

The Turkish sun is very hot and can damage young skin easily. Always ensure children wear a high-factor sun cream. Reapply this regularly, especially after they have been in the water.

Limit the time children spend in the sun, especially from noon through the early afternoon when it is at its strongest. Make sure they wear a hat and always carry a lightweight but long-sleeved garment for them in case shoulders and arms need covering up.

Keep children well hydrated – they may not complain of feeling thirsty but will need lots of liquid to keep them well.

Sports & Activities

GOLF

The courses at Belek (see page 46) offer the most varied quality golf in the eastern Mediterranean. There is professional instruction for all ages and standards, plus a practice driving range and 9-hole courses where you can improve your stroke play.

WALKING & HIKING

The rugged and unspoiled landscapes of Mediterranean Turkey can really be appreciated on foot. There are several really good footpaths to follow – the best are to Selge from the Köprülü Canyon (see page 62), at Olymbos to the Chimaera flames (see page 75) and along the ridge of the Olymbos Mountain range west of Antalya. Remember to take lots of water and snacks with you. Wear a hat and sensible footwear.

WATER SPORTS

You will not be short of organized water sports unless you choose a particularly quiet resort. From jet skiing to banana boat rides, there is something for all the family at the main resort beaches.

SCUBA DIVING

The warm, clear waters around the Turkish coast make for great diving, but because of the wealth of ancient remains lying in the coastal shallows, many locations remain off limits and divers must be accompanied by registered Turkish guides or dive masters. If you are already qualified, bring your certification with you to enable you to book a guide.

If you want to learn to dive, most large resorts have schools accredited by a Professional Association of Diving Instructors (PADI), where you can be assured of good-quality training.

Many schools also offer taster sessions for people who have never dived before. After a little instruction you are allowed to do a dive under strict supervision – this is a great introduction to the sport.

BOAT TRIPS

A huge flotilla of boats offers day trips and these are good value for money, with lunch and drinks included. It could be to a remote beach or a historic site, but all offer delightful panoramic views of the Turkish coastline and a chance to spot a dolphin or a turtle. The most popular are the trip to Olymbos (see page 74) and the trip to Manavgat Falls (see page 36). It pays to do a little research and price comparison. Check out what is included in the price before making a decision. Tickets usually need to be booked the day before.

CLIMBING

There are excellent climbing opportunities to be found in the Taurus Mountains and the western Lycian peaks to the north and west of Antalya. However, there are no climbing schools to offer lessons, so climbing is not recommended for beginners. For more details, contact the **British Mountaineering Club**. ⓐ 177-179 Burton Road Manchester, M20 2BB ⓣ 0870 010 4878 ⓦ www.thebmc.co.uk

WINDSURFING

Expert windsurfers flock to the Aegean Coast of Turkey for the best conditions, but most resorts on the Mediterranean coast have small schools offering lessons and board rentals. The gentler winds certainly suit the beginner and the improver. Kite surfing is a sport that is growing in popularity.

⬤ *Rock climbing is popular*

Festivals & events

Turkey's festivals and events reflect its fascinating and unique society. A secular republic, it is very proud of its fight for independence, marking the major events with great solemnity. However, over 90 per cent of its population are Muslim, so they also celebrate the main Islamic festivals, especially in the countryside. On top of this, Turkey holds a whole host of sporting competitions and folkloric festivals.

CIVIL CELEBRATIONS

23 April National Sovereignty and Children's Day celebrate the establishment of the first Grand National Assembly in 1920, which saw the end of the Ottoman Empire.

19 May Atatürk Day and Youth and Sports Day mark the beginning of the Turkish War of Independence in 1919, when Atatürk rallied the country to fight the forces who had divided Turkish territory after World War I.

30 August Victory Day celebrates the success of Turkish forces over the Greek army in 1922.

29 October Republic Day marks the date when the present Turkish Republic was declared in 1923.

10 November Atatürk's Death: although not a holiday, Turks mark the day of Atatürk's death in a very poignant way. At 09.05 hours on 10 November, the exact time of his death, the whole country comes to a standstill for a minute of silent remembrance.

MAJOR MUSLIM CELEBRATIONS

The Muslim calendar runs on a lunar cycle different to our solar Gregorian calendar. These celebrations change date each year.

Ramazan (Ramadan)

For the entire ninth month (30 days) of the Muslim year, Muslims fast between dawn and dusk. This marks the time when Mohammed wandered in the desert and Allah revealed the verses of the Koran to him. Muslims devote Ramazan to prayer, reflection and charity.

Şeker Bayramı (She-ker Bay-ramer or the Sugar Festival)

This three-day festival celebrates the end of Ramazan. Families party together and enjoy traditional foods, particularly sugary foods such as *baklava*, pastries and *lokum*.

Kurban Bayramı

The festival that commemorates the prophet Abraham offering his son Isaac to Allah or God (when Allah accepted the sacrifice of a sheep instead). It takes place during the tenth month of the Muslim year.

Other Muslim festivals

Other major and minor festivals are not necessarily holidays but are the times for special prayers and family get-togethers, including:

Aşure Günü (ah-shoo-reh gew-new) The tenth day of the Islamic lunar month of Muharrem commemorates Adam repenting his sin, the birth of the Prophet Abraham, Jonah's deliverance from the whale and the martyrdom of Islamic hero Hüseyin. Also, Turks celebrate Noah's ark coming to rest on dry land.

Mevlid-i Nebi (mehv-leed ee neh-bee) The Prophet Mohammed's birthday is celebrated with mosque illuminations and special foods.

Three other days of celebration where mosques are decorated and lit up are: **Regaip Kandili**, the 'Beginning of the Three Moons'; **Berat Kandili**, the 'Day of Forgiveness'; and **Miraç Kandili**, celebrating the Prophet Mohammed's ascent into heaven.

Circumcision ceremonies

Circumcision is an important milestone in the life of a young Turkish boy and takes place at any time between birth and the age of seven. The child is dressed in new clothes – often a bright satin suit and a light blue headdress – and then paraded around the town visiting family and friends. This was traditionally on horseback but today could be in a parade of cars that travels the streets with horns blaring. After the ceremony there is a big family party.

OTHER FESTIVALS & EVENTS IN THE MEDITERRANEAN REGION

June
- During late June and early July the **Aspendos Opera and Ballet Festival** runs a programme of international works featuring the crème de la crème of the performing world, performed in the Roman theatre at Aspendos (see page 60).

July
- Aspendos is again the focus for the **Aspendos Folk Festival** featuring traditional Turkish music and dance.

August
- Alanya hosts an **International Folklore Festival** featuring mainly Turkish and Eastern Mediterranean music and dance.

October
- Antalya welcomes the cinematographic industry to the **Antalya Altın Portakal Film Festival (Golden Orange Film Festival)**, probably the most important in the eastern Mediterranean basin. International arts-type films are featured.

- Alanya holds an **International Triathlon** – with swimming, cycling and running on a route through the city.

PRACTICAL INFORMATION
Tips & advice

Preparing to go

GETTING THERE

Turkey is a popular destination and features in the brochures of all the major package tour operators with a range of hotels and holidays in all price brackets. Prices are highest when demand is high, such as during school holiday periods, when it is wise to book as early as possible, especially if you have children.

If you are more flexible, it will be less busy and cheaper to travel early (May/June) or late in the season (September/October), when last-minute bargains are possible. Teletext, the Internet or travel agents offer ways to compare prices and facilities whatever time of year you want to travel. If you want to organize your own package you can book a scheduled flight (flexible dates) or charter flight (fixed dates of one or two weeks' duration) and find your own accommodation. Many hotels have their own websites that allow you to make and confirm booking, or use specialist companies such as **Expedia** (www.expedia.co.uk), **Travelocity** (www.travelocity.co.uk) or **Priceline** (www.priceline.co.uk).

You should also check the travel supplements of the weekend newspapers such as the *Sunday Telegraph* and *Sunday Times*. They often carry adverts for inexpensive flights and privately owned villas and apartments to rent.

By air

You will fly into **Antalya International Airport** when you travel to the Mediterranean resorts. This is in the east of the region with the longest transfers to Alanya (approximately 3 hours). The airport caters to charter flights from many UK airports during the holiday season (April–October).

There are no direct international scheduled flights to Antalya. You need to take a flight into Istanbul and then fly onwards with **Turkish Airlines**, the national carrier. It operates several flights a day throughout the year.

The airport has duty-free shops, exchange bureaux, car-rental offices and taxis, but services are limited if you arrive or depart at night.

TOURIST INFORMATION

For more information about Turkey before you leave, contact the
Turkish Culture and Tourism Office @ 170–173 Piccadilly, London W1J 9EJ
📞 0207 629 7771 📠 0207 491 0773 🌐 www.gototurkey.co.uk

BEFORE YOU LEAVE

Holidays are supposed to be relaxing, so take a little time and plan
ahead. You do not need inoculations to travel to Turkey but it would be
wise to make sure that your family is up to date with shots like tetanus.
It is also worth having a dental check-up before you go.

It is sensible to carry a small first-aid kit with items such as
painkillers, treatment for upset stomachs, travel/sea-sickness tablets,
plasters, antiseptic ointment and insect repellent. Sun cream is more
expensive in Turkey, so buy this before you go. If you take any prescription
medication make sure you have enough for the duration of your holiday.

DOCUMENTS

The most important documents you will need are tickets and passports.
Make sure that passports for all members of the family are up to date.
Children already named on a parent's passport can travel without their
own passports, but any recent additions to the family or children not
on a passport already will need to have their own. These can take up to
28 days to be issued by the passport office, although you can pay more
for a quicker service. If your passport has less than three months to run
on the date you arrive in Turkey, you need to renew it before you go.
For further information on how to renew you passport and for current
processing times, get in touch with the **Passport Agency** (📞 0870 521
0410 🌐 www.ukpa.gov.uk). When your tickets arrive from the travel
agent check that all the names, dates and times are correct.

Keep passports and travel tickets or confirmations in a safe place.
If possible keep photocopies of your passport numbers and ticket
information (and travellers' cheques if you take them) separately.

If you are going to hire a car while in Turkey all named drivers need
to have their driver's licences with them.

MONEY

Always change a small amount of currency before you leave, especially if your flight arrives late in the evening or early in the morning. You can do this at a post office, travel agent (allow two or three days for the money to arrive) or at the airport just before you fly. Make sure that your credit and debit cards are up to date before you travel.

Changing money Banks can be found in all major towns. There are plenty of exchange bureaux in resorts. Before you change money check the exchange and commission rates. You will find cashpoints in the larger resorts, but not all smaller resorts.

Travellers' cheques These provide the safest way to carry money since they can be replaced if lost or stolen (remember to note down the cheque numbers in the event of needing to have them replaced). Order them from a bank or travel agent at least a week before you leave on holiday. Travellers' cheques can be cashed at banks, exchange bureaux and many hotels.

ATM machines These are widespread in the resort areas. You can obtain cash with either your Maestro Card or credit card provided you have a Personal Identification Number (PIN). Your bank or credit card company may charge more for this service.

Credit cards These are becoming more widely accepted in shops and restaurants but not in cheaper *lokantas* and *pide* stalls or in the markets, so do not rely on this as your only method of payment.

 You can often pay in pounds rather than in Turkish Lira, so it pays to take some British cash; remember to keep this secure.

INSURANCE

Check that your insurance policy covers you adequately for loss of possessions and valuables, for activities you might want to try – such as horse-riding or water sports – and for emergency medical and dental treatment, including flights home, if required. Note also that UK visitors are not entitled to reduced-cost or free medical treatment, as Turkey is not, at the time of writing, a part of the EEA.

CLIMATE

The coastal areas of western Turkey have a Mediterranean climate. This means long, hot dry summers, mild winters with some rain and short, warm springs and autumns.

Average daytime temperatures are: April – 20°C (68°F); May – 24°C (75°F); June – 29°C (84°F); July – 31°C (88°F); August – 32°C (90°F); September – 29°C (84°F); October – 24°C (75°F).

In summer you will only need light clothing – breathable and natural fabrics are best – but take lightweight trousers and a long-sleeved shirt to cover your arms and legs in case you get sunburnt.

Early or late in the season take a warmer layer like a light fleece just in case it gets a bit chilly in the evenings.

PETS

Make sure your pets are cared for while you are away. A neighbour may come in to feed them, or book larger animals such as cats or dogs into a pet hotel. These can be full in summer, so make reservations early.

SECURITY

Take sensible precautions to prevent your house being burgled while you are away:

- Cancel milk, newspapers and other regular deliveries so that post and milk does not pile up on the doorstep, indicating that you are away.
- Let the postman know where to leave parcels and bulky mail (ideally with a next-door neighbour) that will not go through your letterbox.
- If possible, arrange for a friend or neighbour to visit regularly, closing and opening curtains in the evening and morning, and switching lights on and off to give the impression that the house is being lived in.
- Consider buying electrical-timing devices that will switch lights and radios on and off, again to give the impression that there is someone in the house.

- Let Neighbourhood Watch representatives know that you will be away so that they can keep an eye on your home.
- If you have a burglar alarm, make sure that it is serviced and working properly and is switched on when you leave (you may find that your insurance policy requires this). Ensure that a neighbour is able to gain access to the alarm to turn it off if it is set off accidentally.
- If you are leaving cars unattended, put them in a secure garage, if possible, and leave a key with a neighbour in case the alarm goes off.

SPECIAL MEALS

Do not forget that you need to book special in-flight meals (for example vegetarian, vegan or diabetic) well in advance – preferably when the booking is made, but otherwise at least two weeks in advance of your departure.

AIRPORT PARKING & ACCOMMODATION

Book airport parking or overnight accommodation close to the airport as soon as you have booked your holiday. Demand for both is high, especially in the summer. Some hotels offer free parking for a one- or two-week holiday if you book rooms with them.

BAGGAGE ALLOWANCES

Baggage allowances are becoming more strict and the price of excess baggage (that over the amount allowed as part of your ticket) is expensive. Currently scheduled flights allow 20 kg (44 lb) of checked-in baggage (bags that go into the hold) per passenger, but charter flights have lower limits, as little as 15 kg (33 lb) for clients who have booked at the last minute or bought a flight-only package. Your tour company will tell you your limit and it will be printed on your ticket. Each passenger is also allowed to carry a small bag (5 kg/11 lb) onto the plane, plus duty-free shopping and items such as laptop computers and cameras.

If you think you may want to take more than this allowance, ask about buying extra baggage capacity before you travel (preferably at the same time as you book your ticket). Many airlines can sell extra capacity to you that will be much less expensive than would be the case if you just turned up at the check-in desk with overweight bags.

If you are going to be travelling with a large item – a push-chair, golf clubs or surf board, for example – let the holiday company know when you make the booking. There may be an extra charge for these.

CHECK-IN, PASSPORT CONTROL & CUSTOMS

For first-time travellers, airport procedures and security can be a little intimidating but the process is simple and straightforward.

Check-in desks usually open two or three hours before a flight is scheduled to leave. Leave the house so that you arrive early at the airport. This will give you a good choice of seat and help avoid any unforeseen delay en route that will make you miss your flight. Most airports have good restaurant and café facilities and it is better to wait in them for your flight time rather than to stress over being late. You can always use this time to read up on your holiday destination.

Look for your flight number on the TV monitors in the check-in area and find the relevant check-in desk. Your tickets will be checked and your luggage taken. Take your boarding card and go to the departure lounge through the security check area. Here your hand luggage will be x-rayed and your passport checked.

In the departure lounge, you can still shop for duty-free goods, but watch the monitors that tell you when to board – usually about 30 minutes before take-off. Go to the departure gate shown and follow the instructions given you by the airline staff.

Because Turkey is outside the EU, you will be allowed to purchase goods 'duty free'. You will not be allowed to take more than the following amounts of duty-free goods into Turkey.

- 200 cigarettes or 50 cigars or 200g of tobacco
- 5 litres (9 pt) of alcohol

During your stay

AIRPORTS

There is good road access to the region's airports, but if you are returning
a rental car at the end of your holiday allow plenty of time to reach
the airport and check in for your flight. If your flight departs at night,
the airport will have limited facilities during your wait, so it might be
wise to take drinks and snacks. Also, duty-free shops may not be open
at night.

CURRENCY

In January 2005, Turkey devalued its currency and issued new notes
and coins. The Yeni (New) Turkish Lira or YTL replaced the old Turkish Lira,
and each new Lira is worth 1,000,000 old Lira. Yeni Lira come in note
denominations of 1, 5, 10, 20, 50 and 100 Lira. Each Yeni Lira is made up
of 100 Kuruş, which come in coins of 1, 5, 10, 25 and 50 Kuruş. There is also
a 1 Lira coin.

ELECTRICITY

Power is 220 volts, 50 cycles. Plugs are European style with 2 round pins
so you will need an adapter for your electrical appliances.

EMBASSIES & CONSULATES

The British Embassy ⓐ Sehit Ersan Caddesi 46/A, Çankaya, Ankara
❶ 0312 455 3344
British Vice Consulate ⓐ 1314 Sokak 6/8, Genclik Mahallesi, Antalya
❶ 0242 244 5313

TELEPHONING TURKEY
To call Turkey from the UK, dial 00 90 followed by the area code
(without the initial zero), then the 7-digit number that follows.

FACILITIES FOR VISITORS WITH DISABILITIES

Turkey is working hard to improve facilities for the disabled but provision is still patchy. Many newly built hotels and public buildings have facilities but access to archaeological sites and historic buildings is difficult and the lack of curb ramps and controlled street crossings in towns makes movement problematical. If necessary, contact the hotels direct to ensure that they can provide what you need. For further help, contact **Holiday Care International**, who have information about facilities and accessibility in destinations for travellers with disabilities. 🔵 7th Floor, Sunley House, 4 Bedford Park, Croydon, Surrey CR0 2AP 🔵 0845 124 9971 🔵 www.holidaycare.org.uk

GETTING AROUND

Car hire The easiest way to rent a car is to book it in the UK at the same time as you book your holiday. This way you can be clear about costs and correct insurance cover. It is also easy to rent a car in Turkey if you decide you want a couple of days or more on the road. At your resort, your representative will be able to help you, or visit a local car-rental office. Check the quality of the cars before you rent.

You will need to leave a deposit and show your driving licence. For all car rentals, make sure you get a contact telephone number in case you have mechanical problems. Drivers must be over 21 years of age (some companies 25 years) and have held a full licence for at least a year.

Driving In Turkey you drive on the right and overtake on the left (the opposite of the UK). Speed limits are 50 km/h (31 mph) in urban areas, 90 km/h (56 mph) on main roads and 120 km/h (75 mph) on motorways and dual carriageways – unless the signs indicate another limit. Seat belts are compulsory in front seats and back seats where fitted.

The main coast road and other major roads are generally in good condition, but small roads vary in quality and some are dirt surface rather than asphalt. You will meet all kinds of traffic on the roads, from large, modern trucks to donkey and carts (and the occasional loose farm animal). You will need to be on the alert for slower moving vehicles. Slower traffic will usually move onto the hard shoulder to allow you to pass. If Turkish drivers want to cross the traffic, they will often pull over to the right and let traffic behind them pass before making the turn so they do not hold everyone up.

When traffic is quieter (at night and on Sundays), Turkish traffic lights are switched to flashing amber. This means that you will need to pay attention because there is a junction or crossroads ahead that is not controlled.

Parking is a problem in all the major resorts. Do not park where you see a yellow kerb.

You will find both leaded and unleaded petrol. Not all fuel stations are self-service. A member of staff may come and clean your windscreen. This is at no extra cost, but staff will appreciate a small tip. Some petrol stations do not accept credit cards.

Long distance bus services All Turkish towns and cities are served by an efficient, modern and cheap bus network that makes an excellent framework for touring the country. The services include air conditioning, videos (in Turkish, of course), refreshments and pre-programmed stops for meals.

Local buses The dolmuş is the lifeblood of local transport. These small mini-vans run set routes, leaving the terminus when full and picking up passengers anywhere along the route. There will usually be a service from town to the main beaches and resort hotels. They are cheap and efficient.

HEALTH MATTERS

Should you require medical help, most hotels will have a doctor on call but you will be charged for the consultation (you can usually claim this back from your holiday insurance policy).

Hospital If you need to stay in hospital there are clean, though limited, facilities in most large towns, andsmaller clinics in smaller towns. Staff are well trained and most doctors can speak some English. You have to pay for treatment but depending on circumstances this could be organized directly through your insurance company. If you have travelled on a package holiday with a major tour company, your resort representative will be able to offer advice and help.

Pharmacies (Ezcane) Pharmacists in Turkey are highly qualified and most will speak at least some English. They will be able to advise you on treatments for complaints such as minor sunburn, upset tummy, insect bites and diarrhoea. Normal pharmacy opening hours are from 09.00 to 19.00 and there will be a duty pharmacist available in every town.

Water Although tap water is clean, only drink bottled or boiled water.

THE LANGUAGE

Turkish is a relatively new language. It was developed in the 1920s by Kemal Atatürk, the first President of the Turkish Republic, to replace Arabic.

Pronunciation

Turkish uses the Latin alphabet. Every letter in each Turkish word is pronounced, even when there is a double letter. For example, the word *saat* (hour), is pronounced 'sa-at'. All letters are pronounced as in English except the following:

C which is pronounced as a 'j' as in 'Jerry'
Ç which is pronounced 'ch' as is 'chaffinch'
Ğ which is a silent or soft g, it lengthens the sound of the letter before it
I (a dotless ı) and is pronounce 'a' as in the first syllable of 'another'
Ö as in the 'u' in fur
Ş pronounced 'sh' as in 'ship'
Ü pronounced as the French 'tu'

ENGLISH   TURKISH

Useful words & phrases
Hello   *merhaba*
Good morning   *günaydin*

ENGLISH	TURKISH
Good evening	*iyi akşamlar*
Good night	*iyi geceler*
Goodbye (said by those departing)	*allahaısmarladık*
Goodbye (said by those remaining)	*güle güle*
Yes	*evet*
No	*yok or hayir*
Please	*lutfen*
Thank you	*mersi or teşekkur ederim*
Do you speak English?	*Ingilizce biliyormusunuz*
I don't understand	*anlamıyorum*
I understand	*anlıyorum*
I don't know	*bilmiyorum*
The bill	*hesap*

General vocabulary

Bus	*autobüs*
Small local bus	*dolmüş*
Ferry	*feribot*
Port	*limani*
Plane	*uçak*
Airport	*hava limani*
Ladies (toilet)	*bayanlar*
Mens (toilet)	*baylar*
Left	*sağa*
Right	*sola*
Straight ahead	*doşdogru*
How much is this?	*ne kadar or ne kaça*
Money (cash)	*para*
Too expensive	*çok pahalı*
Travellers' cheques	*seyahat çeki*
Do you sell stamps?	*Posta pulu var mı?*
Open	*açik*

ENGLISH	TURKISH
Postage stamp	*pul*
Closed	*kapalı*
Credit card	kredi kartı
Today	*bugün*
Yesterday	*dün*
Tomorrow	*yarın*
Where is?	*nerede*
Mosque	*cami*
Market or bazaar	*çarşı*
Mountain	*dağ*
Street	*sokak* (often abbreviated to *sok*)
Avenue	*caddesi* (often abbreviated to *cad*)
Place	*meydani* (often abbreviated to *meyd*)
Boulevard	*Bulvari* (abbreviated to *Bul*)
Call the police!	*polise haber verin!*
What time is it?	*saat kaç?*
Duty pharmacy	*nöbeçi ezcane*
Doctor	*doktor*
Emergency exit	*imdat Çikişi*
Hospital	*hastane*
Room	*oda*
Toilet	*tuvalet*
Shower	*duş*
Towel	*havlu*

Numbers

One	*bir*
Two	*iki*
Three	*üç*
Four	*dört*
Five	*beş*
Six	*altı*

ENGLISH	**TURKISH** (pronunciation)
Seven	*yedi*
Eight	*sekiz*
Nine	*dokuz*
Ten	*on*
One hundred	*yüz*
One thousand	*bin*

Days of the week

Monday	*pazartezi*
Tuesday	*salı*
Wednesday	*çarşamba*
Thursday	*perşembe*
Friday	*cuma*
Saturday	*cumartesi*
Sunday	*pazar*

LAUNDRY

There are few public laundry facilities in Turkey. Most large hotels offer laundry and dry-cleaning services at a price premium.

LOST PROPERTY

If it is possible, retrace your steps. Turks are honest people by nature and someone may have it in safekeeping for you.

- If you have a rep, report the matter to them and ask their advice.
- Visit the nearest police station to report your loss.
- Report any lost credit cards to the credit-card company immediately.
- Report any lost passport to your nearest embassy or consulate immediately.

MAKING A COMPLAINT

If you want to make a complaint about anything that happens during your holiday, explain as simply as you can what the problem is. Stay calm and do not lose your temper. Your holiday representative is there to help make your holiday as enjoyable as possible. See them for any complaint about your flight or hotel. In restaurants or shops, ask to speak to the manager or owner.

MEDIA

The only English-language newspaper printed in Turkey is the *Turkish Daily News*. The popular English tabloids are widely available in all the leading resorts at a price premium, though they may be a day old. Most upmarket hotels will offer BBC *News 24* as part of their programming. Resort bars will often transmit Premier League matches live, and show English news reports. You will find Internet cafés in most resorts.

OPENING HOURS

Opening hours for museums and archaeological sites change all the time. It is probably best not to arrive too early or too late at a site in case the ticket office is closed. For most places in Turkey, as with the rest of the Mediterranean, it is best to avoid arriving during the lunch hours, as most places will shut for a long lunch. Also be aware of seasonal variations – in the off-season, many places will shut entirely or have reduced hours.

Banks 🕐 08.30–noon and 13.30–17.00 (Mon–Fri)

Shops 🕐 09.00–19.00 (Mon–Sat); tourist shops daily 09.00–22.00 in the resorts in summer

Government offices 🕐 08.30–12.30 and 13.30–17.30 (Mon–Fri)

State museums 🕐 08.30–17.30 (Tues–Sun); closed for lunch in winter

Archaeological sites 🕐 08.00–18.00 or 19.00 in summer.

POST OFFICES

Post offices have yellow signs with the black letters PTT on them. Most post offices are open government office hours and offer postal and telecommunications services. Most shops selling postcards will also sell stamps for a small price premium.

PRACTICAL INFORMATION

PUBLIC TOILETS

There are few public toilet facilities in Turkey. The best policy is to stop
at a café or bar. These are not always of a high standard and
some may be the 'hole in the floor' Continental-type toilets. If in a resort,
visit the nearest hotel. These facilities should be modern and clean.
Always carry a supply of toilet roll or tissue, as few toilets outside the
hotels will have a supply. In museums and archaeological sites you may
have to pay a small amount for use of the facilities. Keep small change
handy for this.

RELIGION

Turkey is a predominantly Muslim country, though it is one of the
most liberal Islamic populations in the world. Alcohol and gambling
are allowed. The countryside is generally more conservative than
the coastal resorts. If you are travelling away from the coast, or wanting
to visit mosques or churches, modest dress would be appropriate
and respectful.

SAFETY & SECURITY

Turkey is a safe country and you are very unlikely to find yourself the
victim of a serious incident. However, petty crime such as theft can be
guarded against with a few simple rules.

- Don't carry large amounts of cash or valuables with you. Take only
  what you need for the day.
- Leave nothing on show in your car.
- Don't leave valuables unguarded on the beach or at cafes.
- Keep to well-lit streets at night.
- If you are unsure of the route back to your hotel or apartment, take
  a taxi.
- Be sure to report any stolen credit cards to the credit-card company
  immediately.
- Report any stolen passport to your nearest embassy or consulate
  immediately.

TELEPHONING ABROAD

To call an overseas number from Turkey, dial 00 followed by the country code (UK=44) and the area code (minus the initial 0), then the rest of the number.

USEFUL TELEPHONE NUMBERS
- **Long distance operator** 131
- **International reverse charge calls** 115
- **International directory enquiries** 161

TELEPHONES

Most resorts have modern public phone boxes that will offer international direct dialling to the UK. These will operate with major credit cards or phone cards that can be purchased at press kiosks, tourist offices and post offices.

Your personal mobile phone should also work, though the cost of calls is a lot higher than local rates at home. Check this with your service provider before you leave.

Most upmarket and resort hotels will offer international direct dialling that will allow you to phone home from your room, but beware of these, as they often charge a high premium. Ask about rates before making the call.

TIME DIFFERENCES

Turkey is two hours ahead of Greenwich Mean Time (GMT) throughout the year.

TIPPING

In restaurants, it is advisable to leave 10–15 per cent of the bill, plus some small change for the waiting staff. In cafés and bars, leave a tip of small change. Bell-boys should receive 50 Kuru (see Currency, page 114) per bag, room cleaners in hotels should be left 50 Kuru per day, and shoe guardians in mosques welcome a small tip.

WEIGHTS & MEASURES

Turkey uses the metric system, so has grams and kilograms, millilitres and litres, metres and kilometres. Use the following conversion table to know the correct weights and measures.

Imperial to metric
1 inch = 2.54 centimetres
1 foot = 30 centimetres
1 mile = 1.6 kilometres
1 ounce = 28 grams
1 pound = 454 grams
1 pint = 0.6 litres
1 gallon = 4.6 litres

Metric to imperial
1 centimetre = 0.4 inches
1 metre = 3 feet, 3 inches
1 kilometre = 0.6 miles
1 gram = 0.04 ounces
1 kilogram = 2.2 pounds
1 litre = 1.8 pints